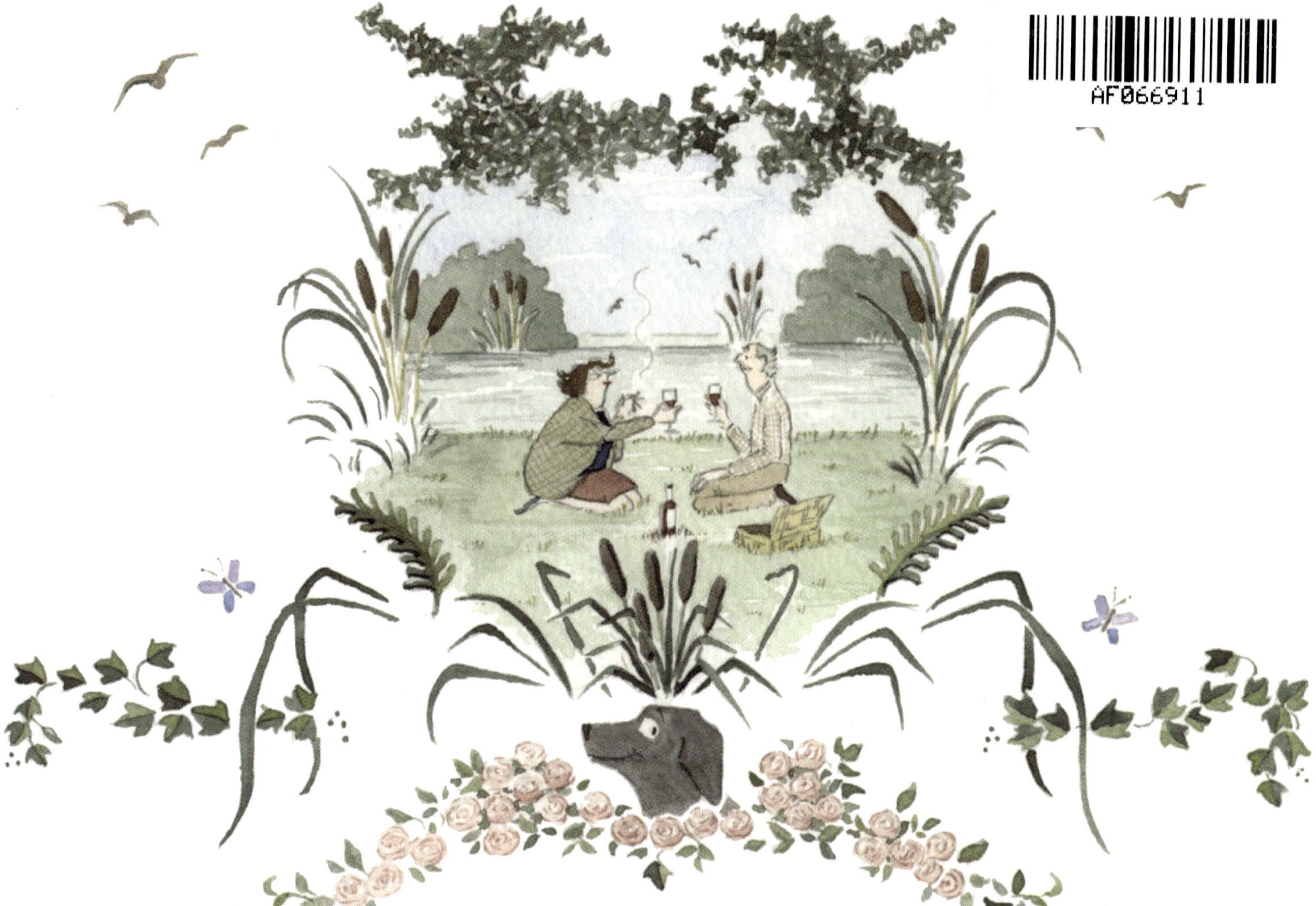

TOTTERING-BY-GENTLY®

Snifters at TOTTERING HALL

ANNIE TEMPEST

Copyright © 2022 The O'Shea Gallery
Text and illustrations copyright © 2022 Annie Tempest
Illustrations archived and compiled by Raymond O'Shea

First published in the UK in 2022 by Quiller,
an imprint of Amberley Publishing

British Library Cataloguing-in-Publication Data
A catalogue record for this book is available from the British Library.

ISBN 978 1 84689 372 8

The right of Annie Tempest to be identified as the author of this work has been asserted in accordance with the Copyright, Design and Patent Act 1988.

All rights reserved. No part of this book may be reproduced or transmitted in any form or by any means, electronic or mechanical including photocopying, recording or by any information storage and retrieval system, without permission from the Publisher in writing.

The images featured in this book are available as prints from www.tottering.com

Printed in China

Quiller
An imprint of Amberley Publishing Ltd
The Hill, Merrywalks, Stroud GL5 4EP
Tel: 01453 847800
Email: info@quillerbooks.com
Website: www.quillerpublishing.com

ANNIE TEMPEST

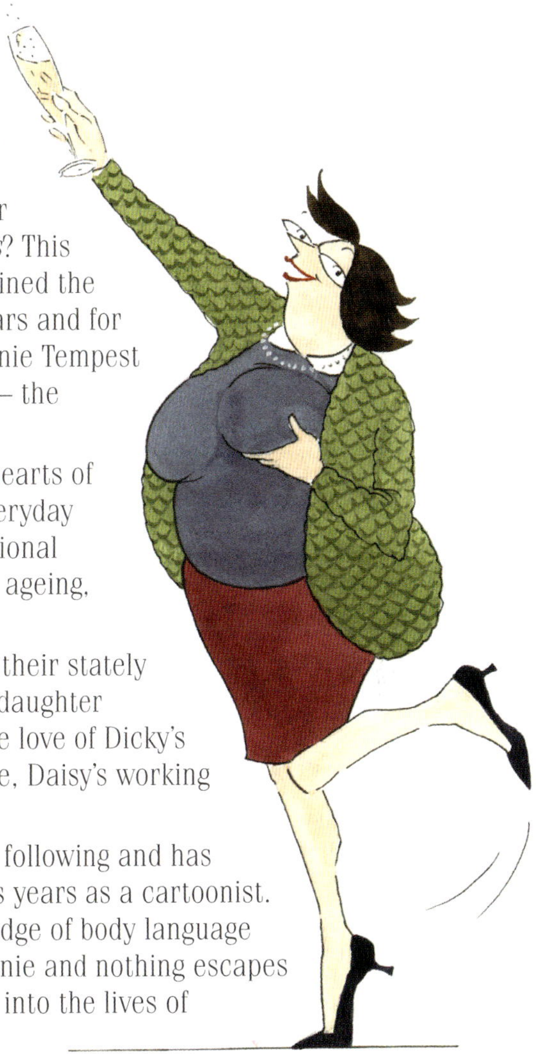

Annie Tempest is one of the top cartoonists working in the UK. This was recognised in 2009 with the Cartoon Art Trust awarding her the Pont Award for the portrayal of the British character. Annie's cartoon career began in 1985 with the success of her first book, *How Green Are Your Wellies*? This led to a regular cartoon, 'Westenders' in the *Daily Express*. Soon after, she joined the *Daily Mail* with 'The Yuppies' cartoon strip which ran for more than seven years and for which, in 1989, she was awarded Strip Cartoonist of the Year. Since 1993 Annie Tempest has been charting the life of Daffy and Dicky Tottering in Tottering-by-Gently – the phenomenally successful weekly cartoon strip in *Country Life*.

Daffy Tottering is a woman of a certain age who has been taken into the hearts of people all over the world. She reflects the problems facing women in their everyday life and is completely at one with herself, while reflecting on the intergenerational tensions and the differing perspectives of men and women, as well as dieting, ageing, gardening, fashion, food, field sports, convention and much more.

Daffy and her husband Dicky live in the fading grandeur of Tottering Hall, their stately home in the fictional county of North Pimmshire, with their extended family: daughter Serena, and grandchildren, Freddy and Daisy. The daily, Mrs Shagpile, and the love of Dicky's life, Slobber, his black Labrador, and the latest addition to the family, Scribble, Daisy's working cocker spaniel, also make regular appearances.

Annie Tempest was born in Zambia in 1959. She has a huge international following and has had numerous one-woman shows all over the world during her thirty-five-plus years as a cartoonist. Over the last decade she has emerged as a sculptor as well, using her knowledge of body language from her years of observation in this new medium. Simply, people interest Annie and nothing escapes her gimlet eye. *Snifters at Tottering Hall* gives Tottering fans another glimpse into the lives of Britain's leading cartoon aristocrats and a chance to raise a glass to them.

INTRODUCTION

When Dicky and Daffy Tottering had their London residence next to Berry Bros & Rudd in St James's Street, they were frequent visitors – both to the shop, and to the Directors' Dining Room above. I got to know them very well and remember thinking after a particularly long and enjoyable lunch that they may be my favourite customers of all. In the top twenty, certainly.

Firstly, they're just as happy ordering Good Ordinary Claret for every day, as First Growth Claret to replace the priceless pre-phylloxera Bordeaux laid down by Dicky's grandfather. And everything in between, as well as port, sherry, champagne, spirits, liqueurs. Dicky mixes a mean Martini, and knows that the only secret ingredient is the best gin possible. They may not be my most adventurous customers – even Italy is a bit of a stretch – but they have adopted bottles with screw caps with gusto ('so useful when the corkscrew's gone AWOL').

Secondly, they both understand, instinctively, that drinking well is one of life's most civilised pleasures. Self-discipline may be required to avoid the fate of Daffy's great-uncle Cuthbert (of whom the least said the better), but not to the extent of succumbing to a Dry January or some other media-created lunacy.

And thirdly: they're great fun, and the most delightful company at the aforementioned lunches. I can mix them with anyone, and know that the conversation will flow. Only one archetype must be avoided: the 'Wine Bore'. But even if one slips through the net, the Totterings are guaranteed to change the subject and lead the conversation down far more enjoyable avenues.

Now that they spend so much more of their time in Pimmshire, I see them less often. So I am delighted to be asked to write this introduction to Annie Tempest's documentary record of their drinking habits. This book will reassure those of us who know that a quick snifter is something to celebrate, not something to hide in shame. And I raise my glass to that.

Simon Berry
Berry Bros & Rudd
3 St James's Street, London SW1

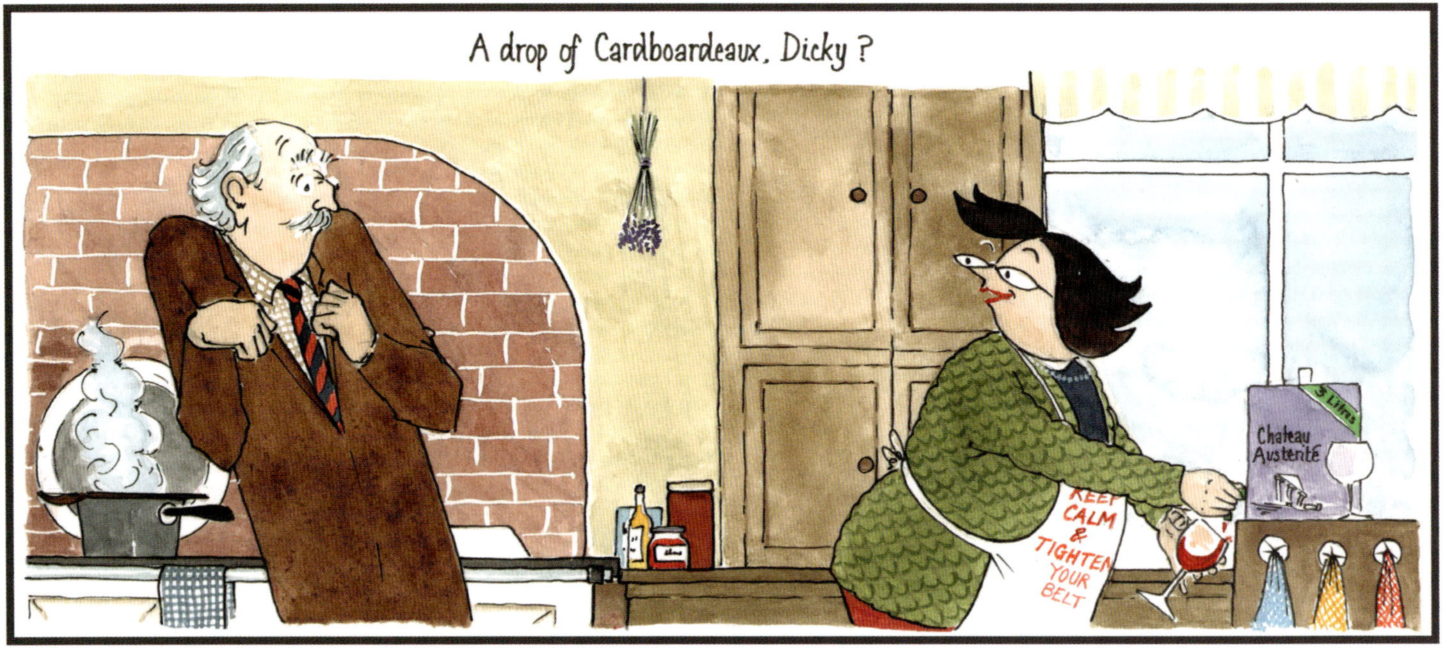
3 Litres
Chateau Austerité
KEEP CALM & TIGHTEN YOUR BELT
A drop of Cardboardeaux, Dicky?

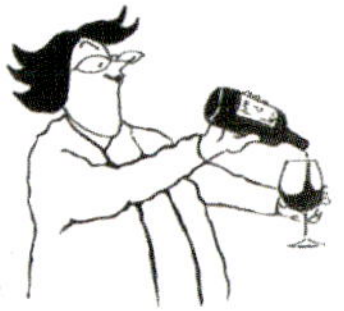

Just being sensible - two glasses each - so we can't touch our faces by accident...

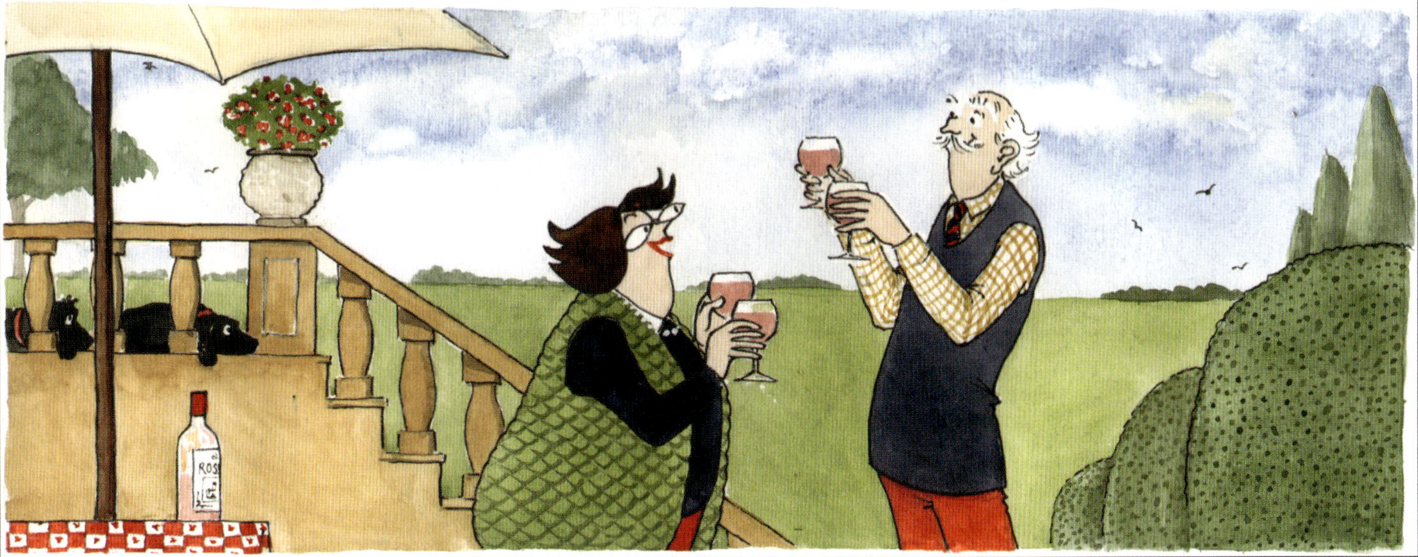

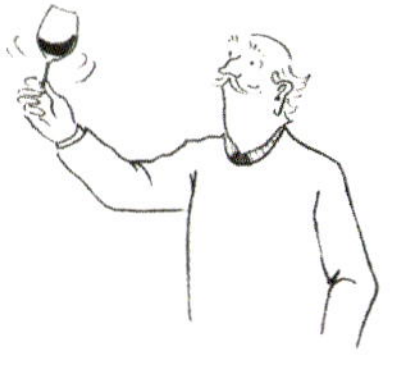

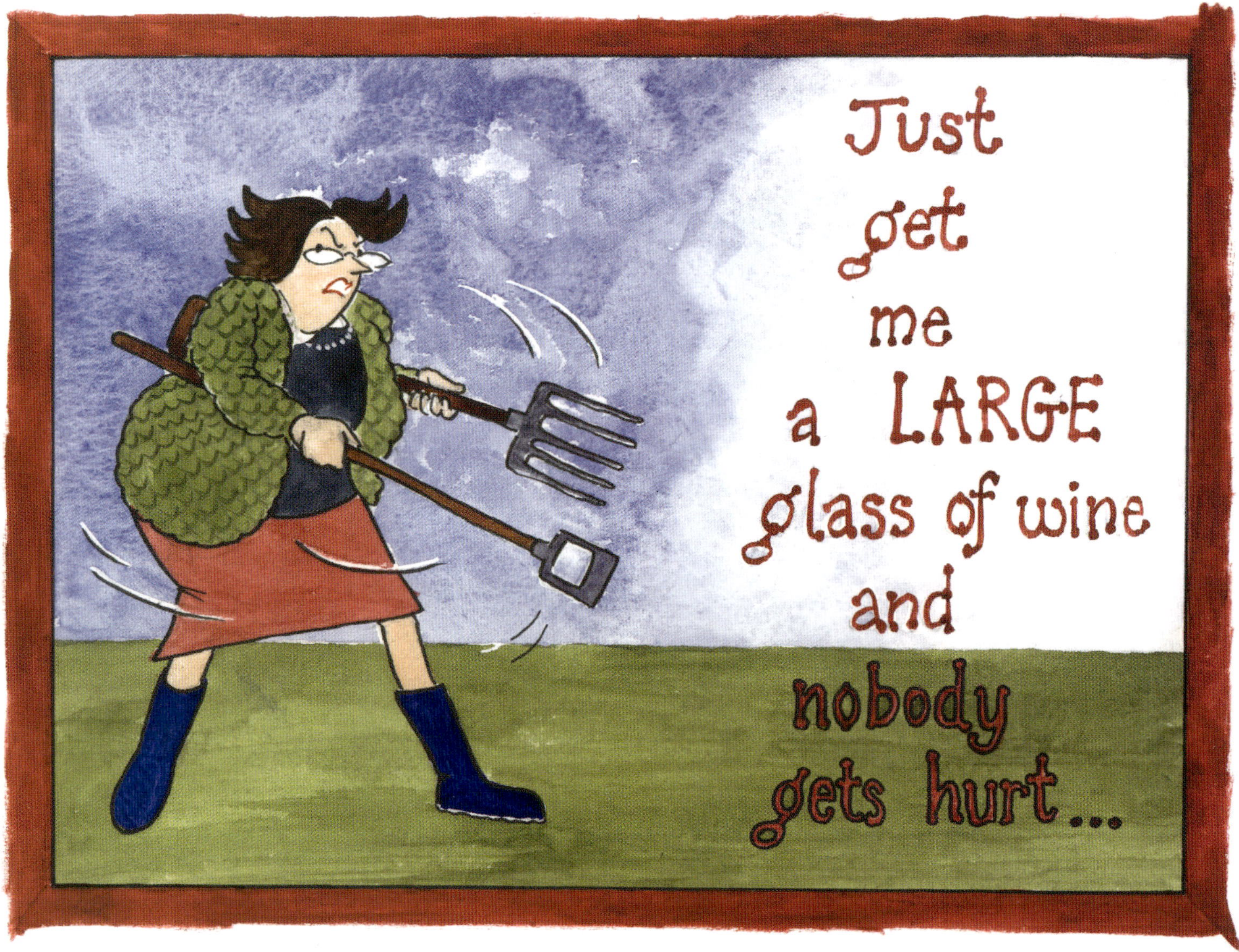
Just get me a LARGE glass of wine and nobody gets hurt...

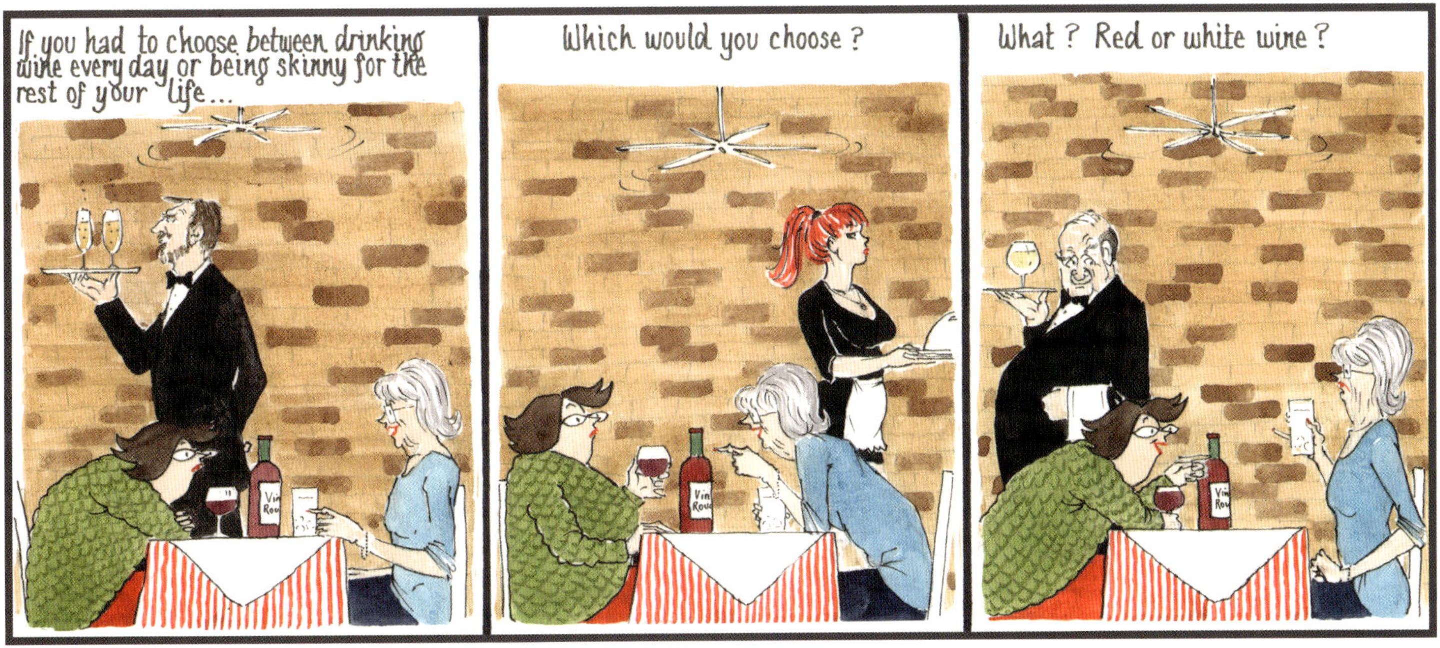
If you had to choose between drinking wine every day or being skinny for the rest of your life...
Which would you choose?
What? Red or white wine?

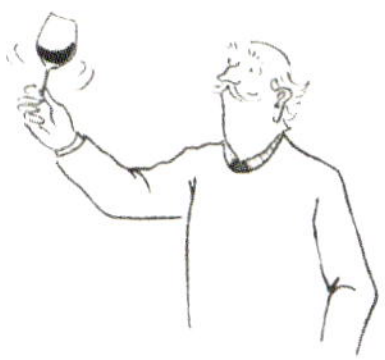

THE FEMALE CHARACTER: A tendency to succumb to a loud 'horizontal life pause' after a second glass of Rosé in the garden ...

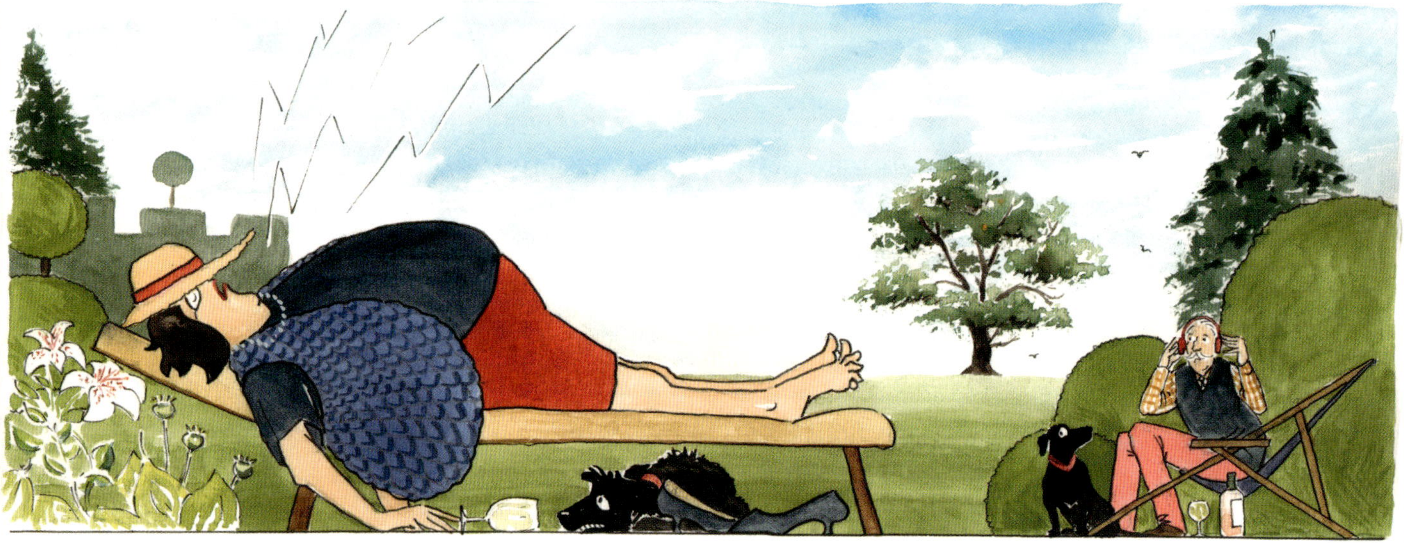

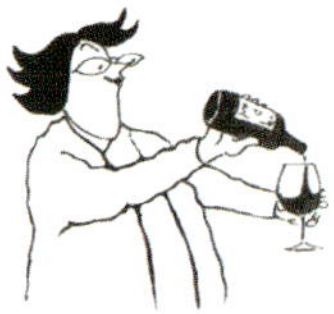

Nooo! Our tunnel is just inches from their cellars!..

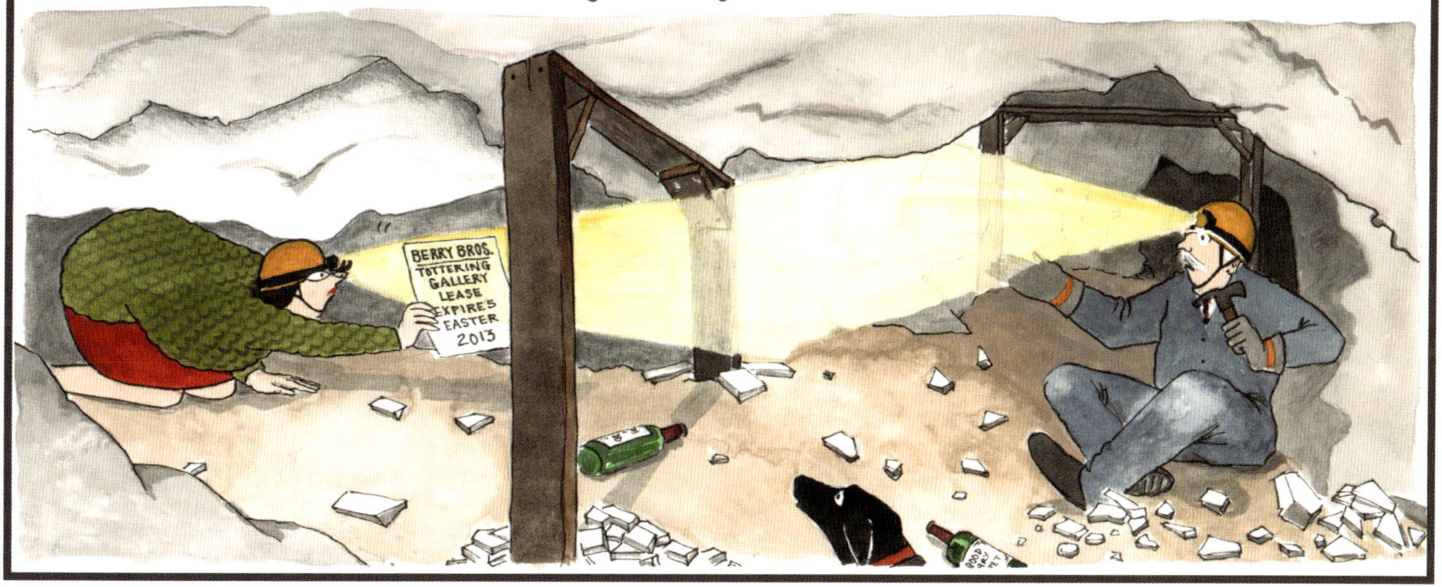
BERRY BROS.
TOTTERING GALLERY LEASE EXPIRE'S EASTER 2013

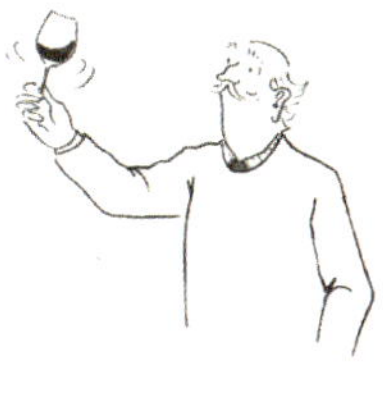

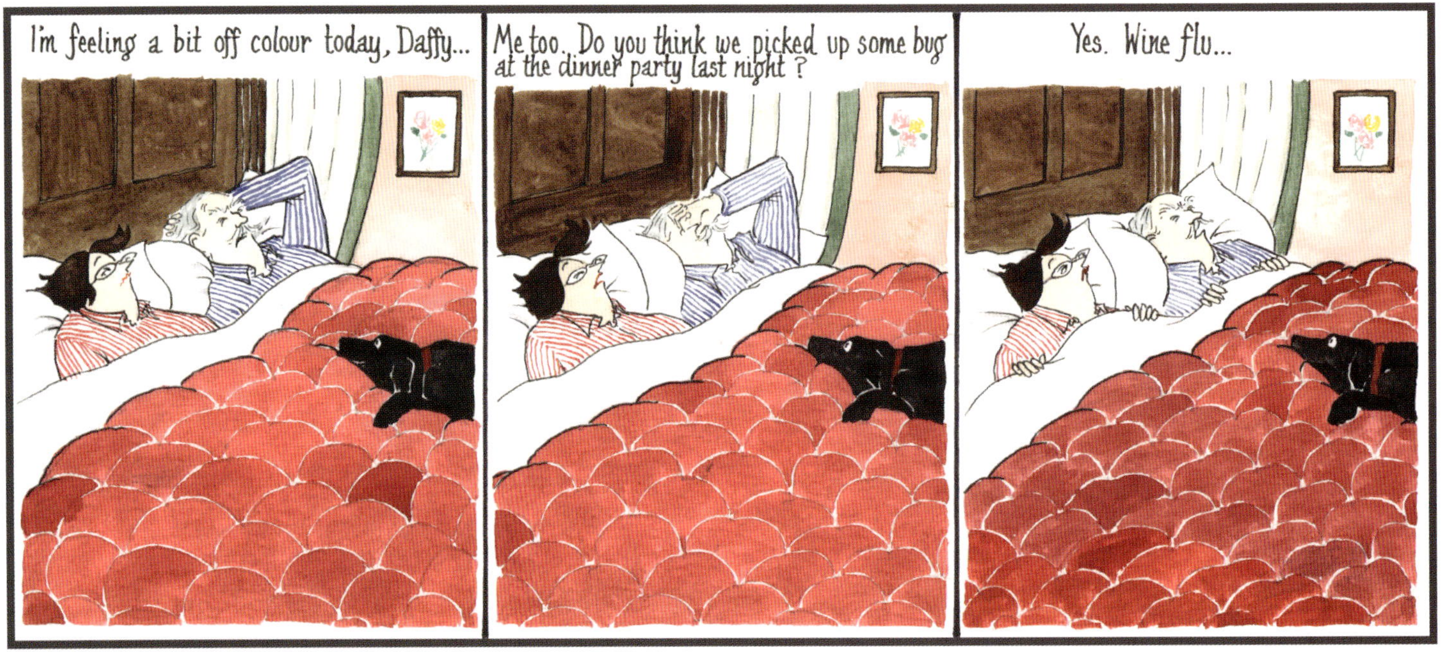
I'm feeling a bit off colour today, Daffy...
Me too. Do you think we picked up some bug at the dinner party last night ?
Yes. Wine flu...

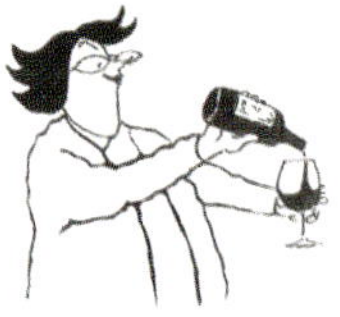

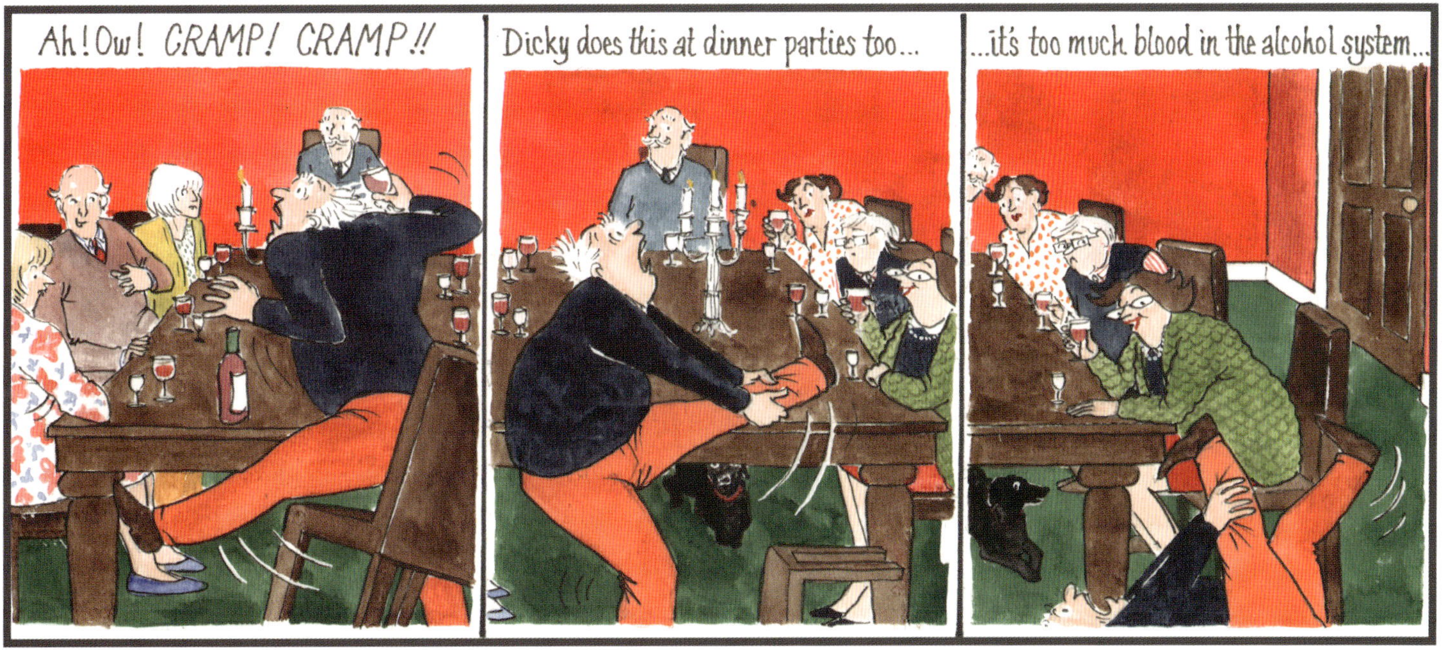
Ah! Ow! CRAMP! CRAMP!!
Dicky does this at dinner parties too...
...it's too much blood in the alcohol system...

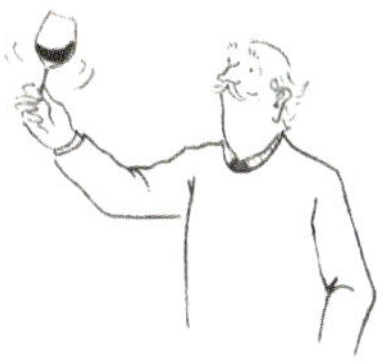

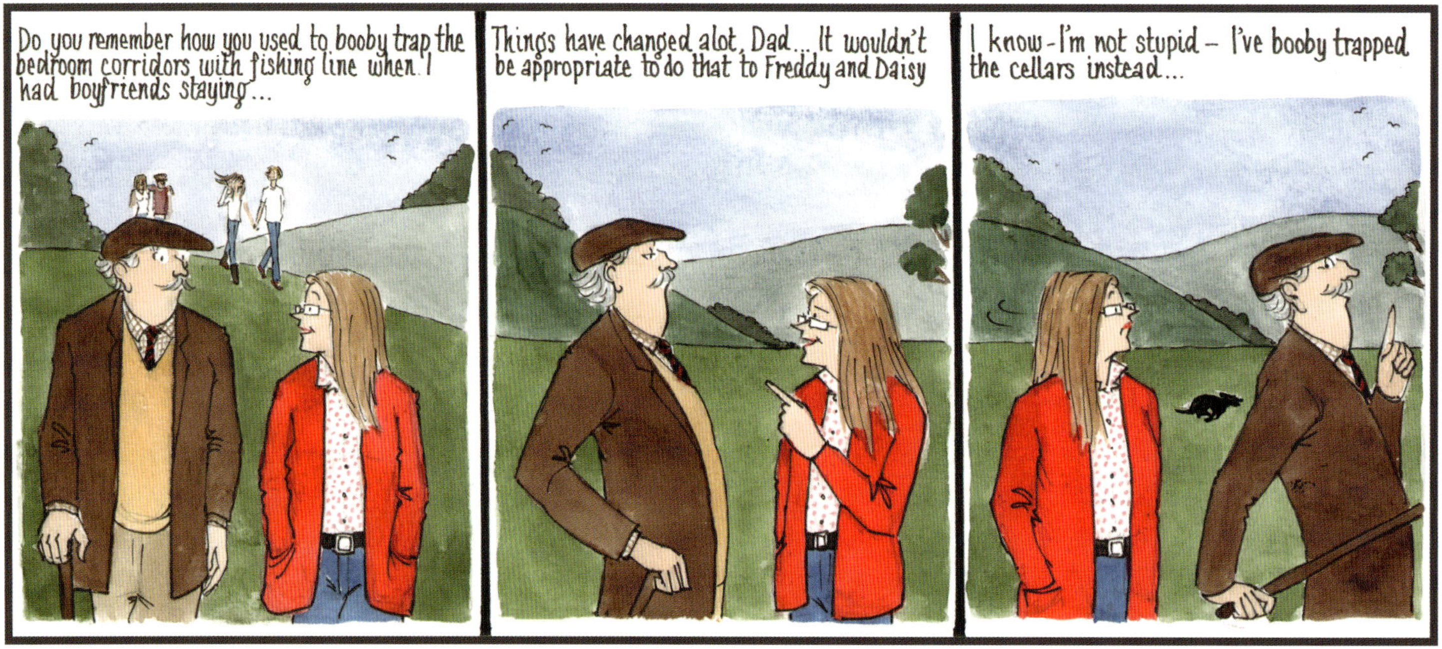
Do you remember how you used to booby trap the bedroom corridors with fishing line when I had boyfriends staying...
Things have changed alot, Dad... It wouldn't be appropriate to do that to Freddy and Daisy
I know - I'm not stupid - I've booby trapped the cellars instead...

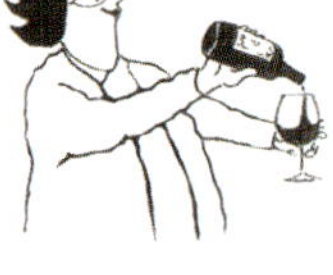

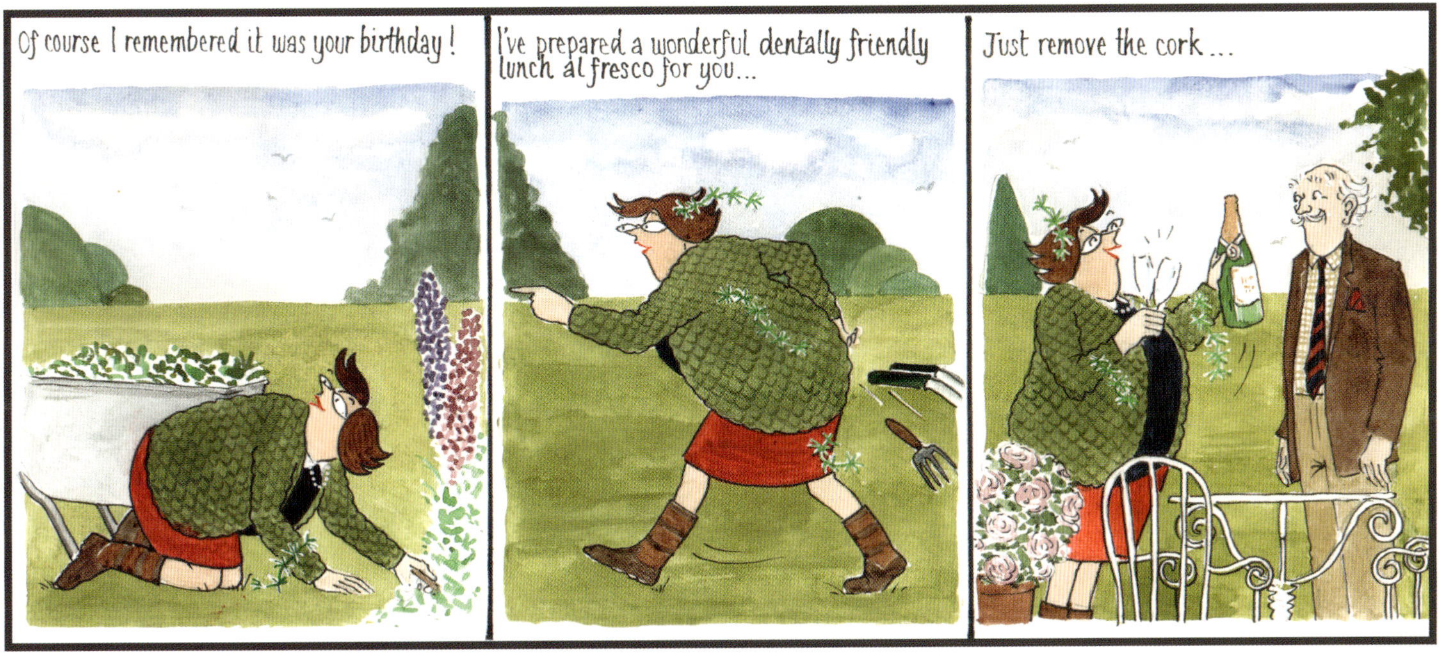
Of course I remembered it was your birthday!
I've prepared a wonderful dentally friendly lunch al fresco for you...
Just remove the cork...

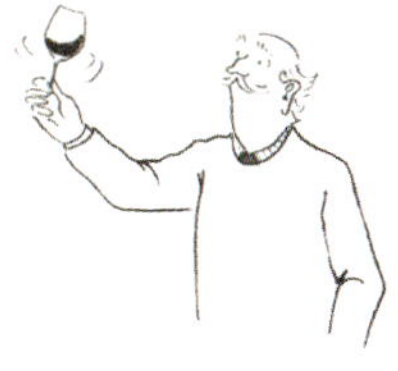

A sure sign of getting older is starting to prefix everything with the word 'little' ...

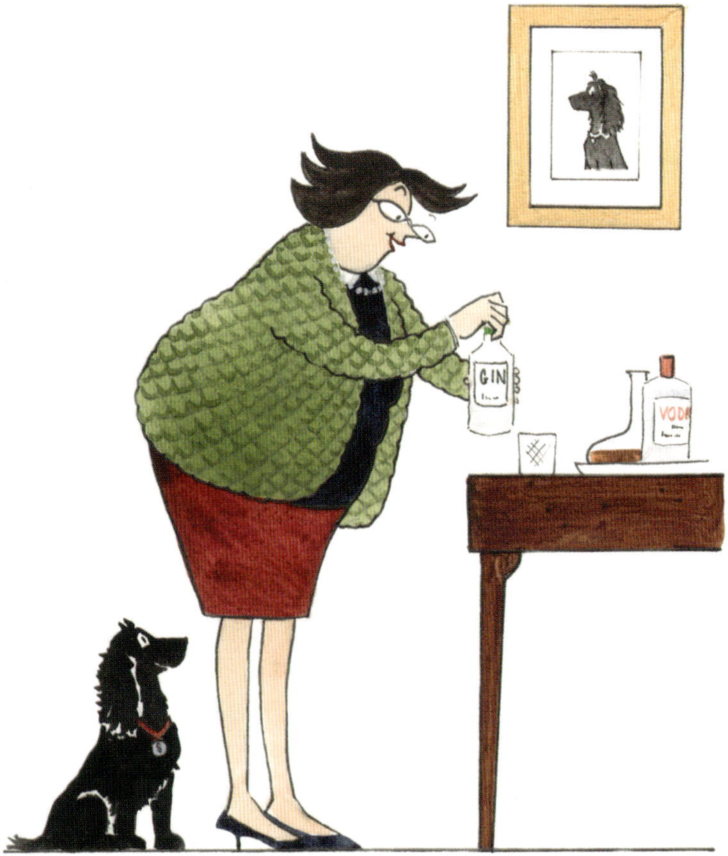
GIN

"Just one more 'little' drop of Gin..."

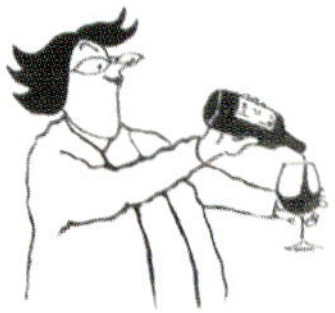

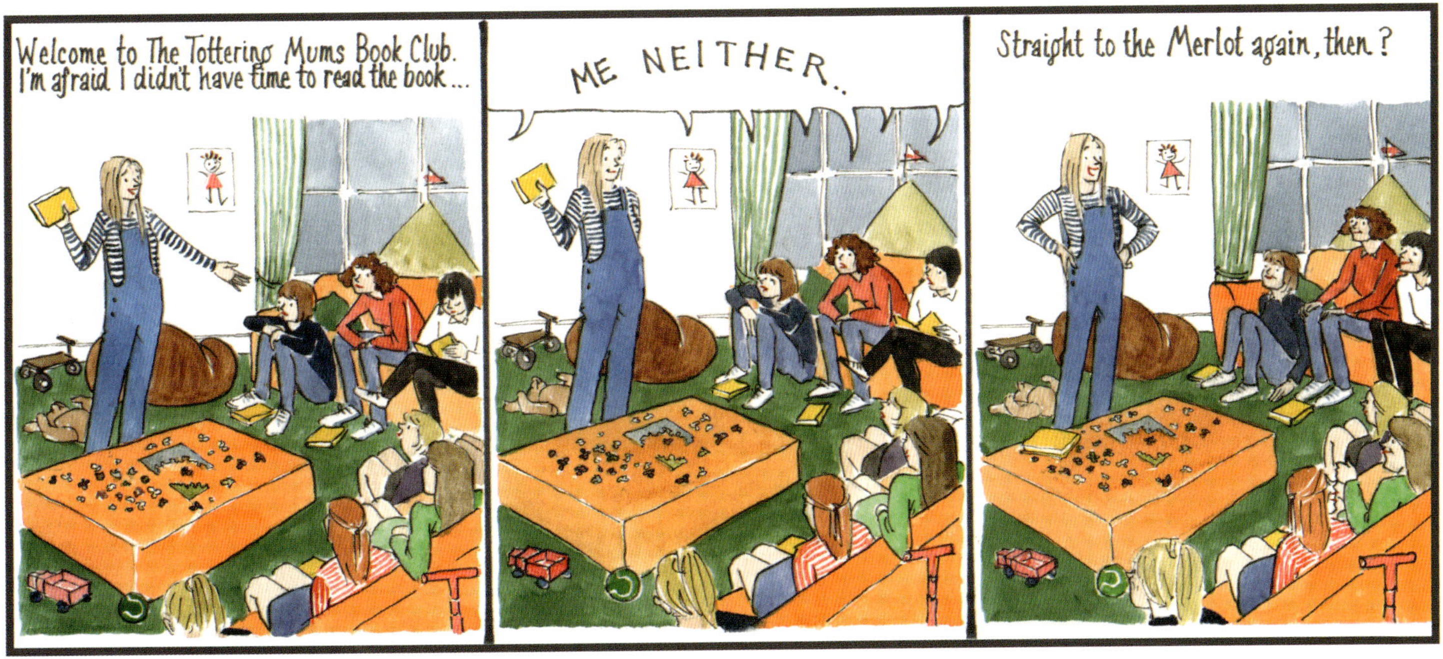
Welcome to The Tottering Mums Book Club.
I'm afraid I didn't have time to read the book...
ME NEITHER..
Straight to the Merlot again, then?

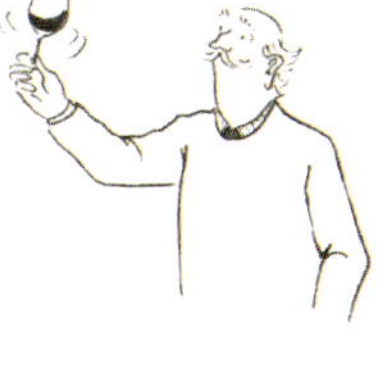

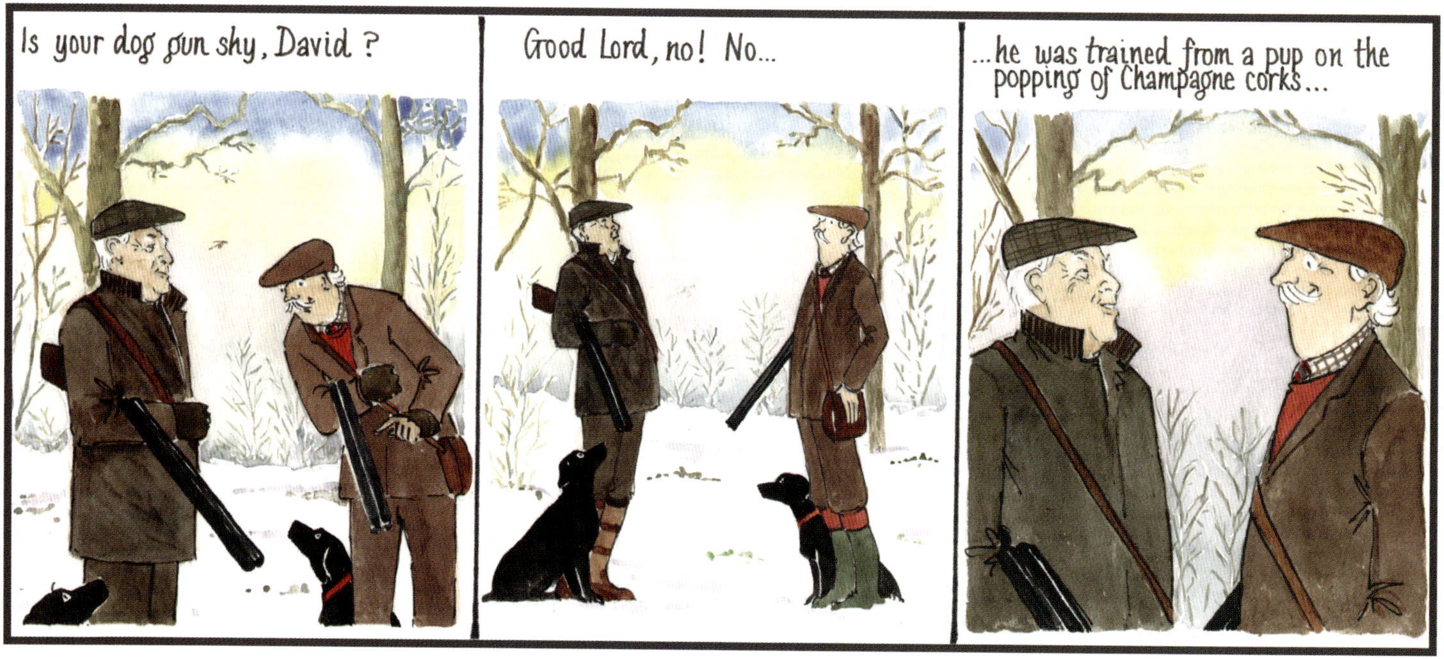
Is your dog gun shy, David?
Good Lord, no! No...
...he was trained from a pup on the popping of Champagne corks...

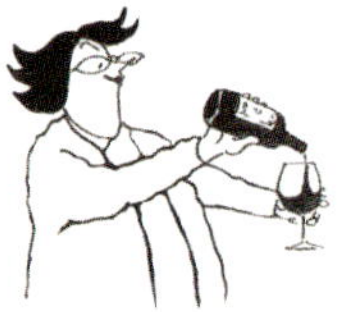

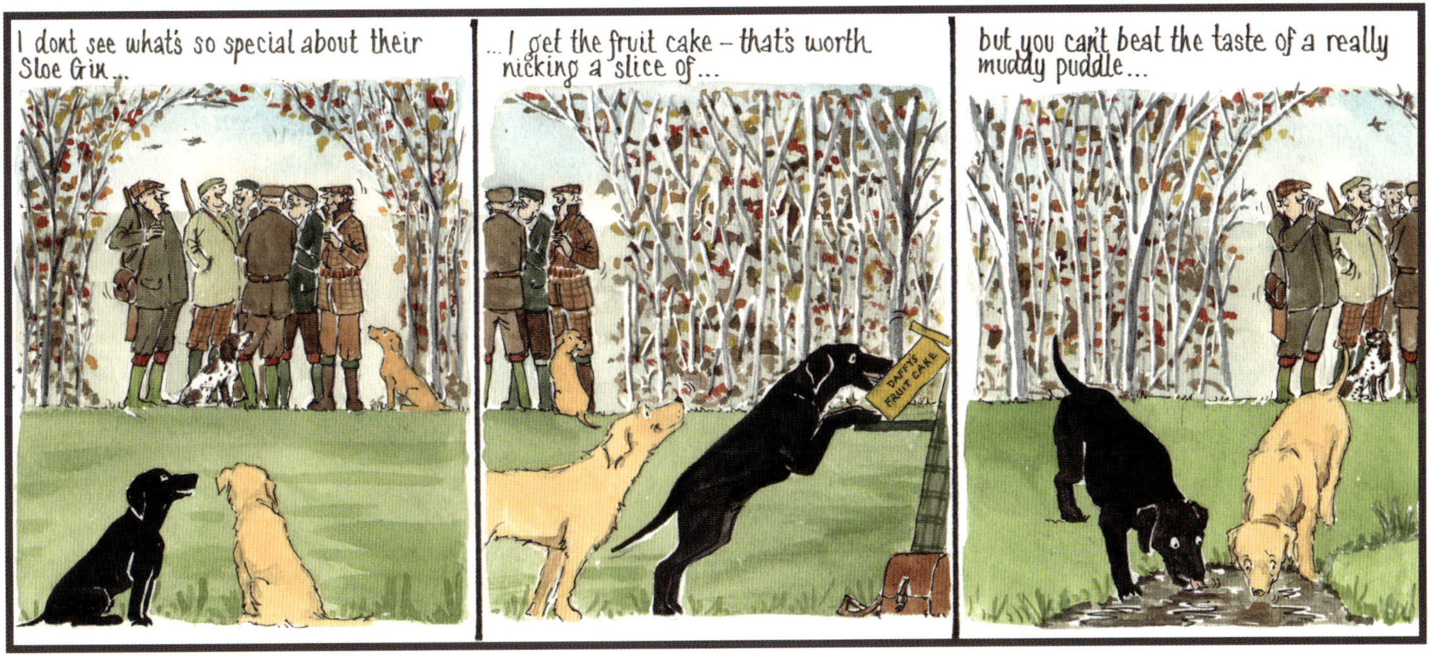
I dont see what's so special about their Sloe Gin...
...I get the fruit cake – that's worth nicking a slice of...
DAFFY'S FRUIT CAKE
but you can't beat the taste of a really muddy puddle...

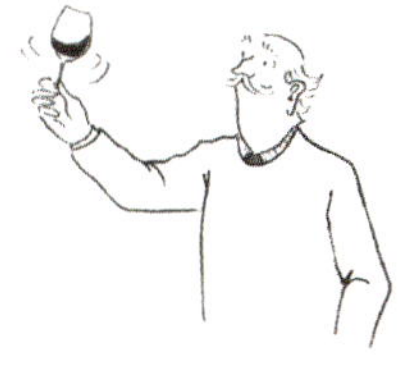

EVEN
GARDENERS
NEED TO TAKE
TIME OUT...

...to
smell
the
roses...

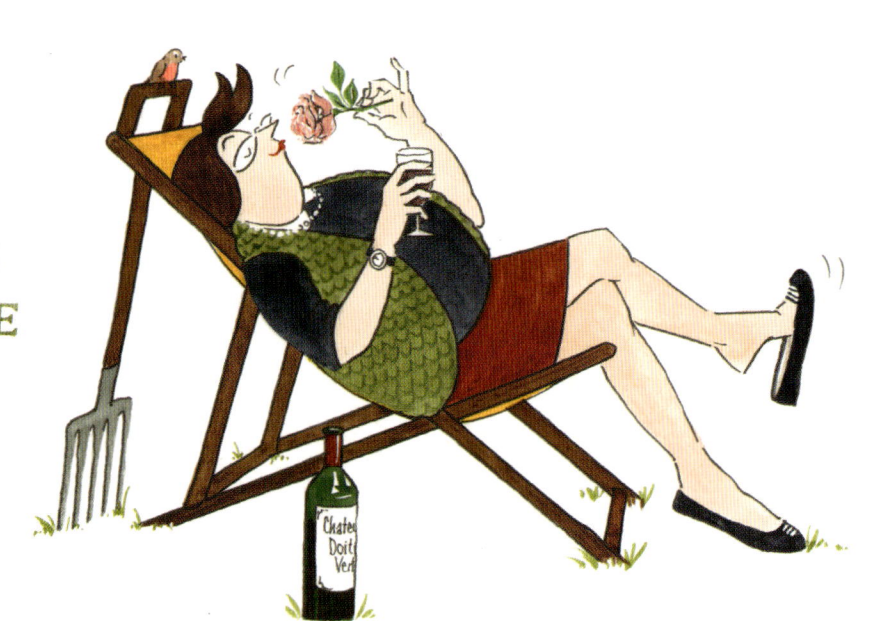

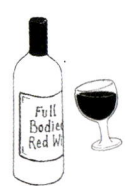

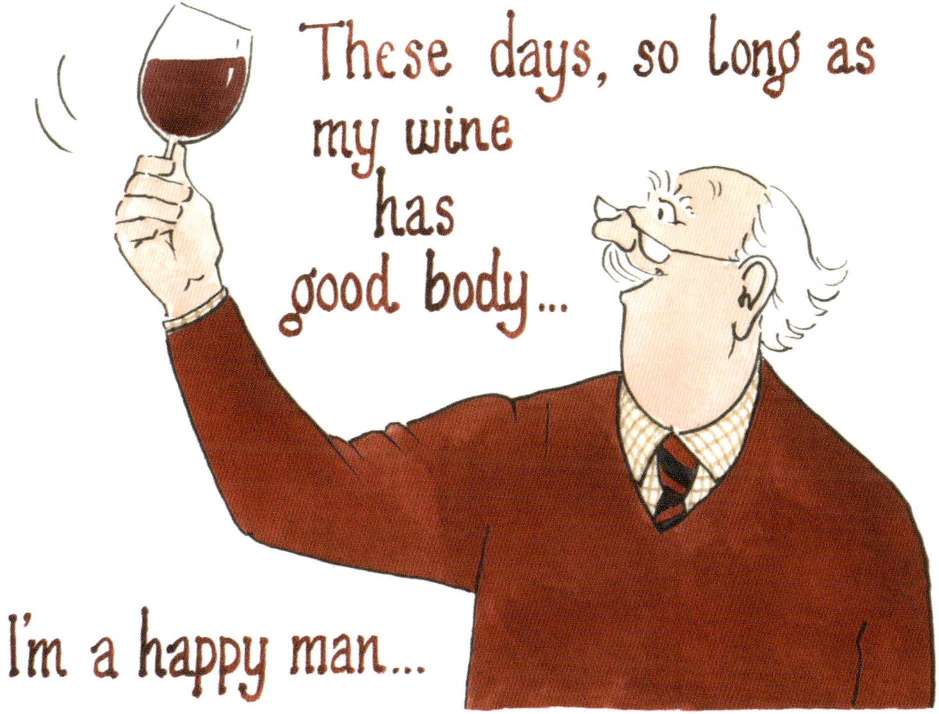
These days, so long as
my wine
has
good body...
I'm a happy man...

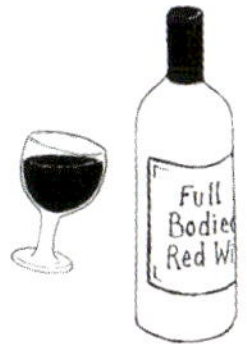
Full

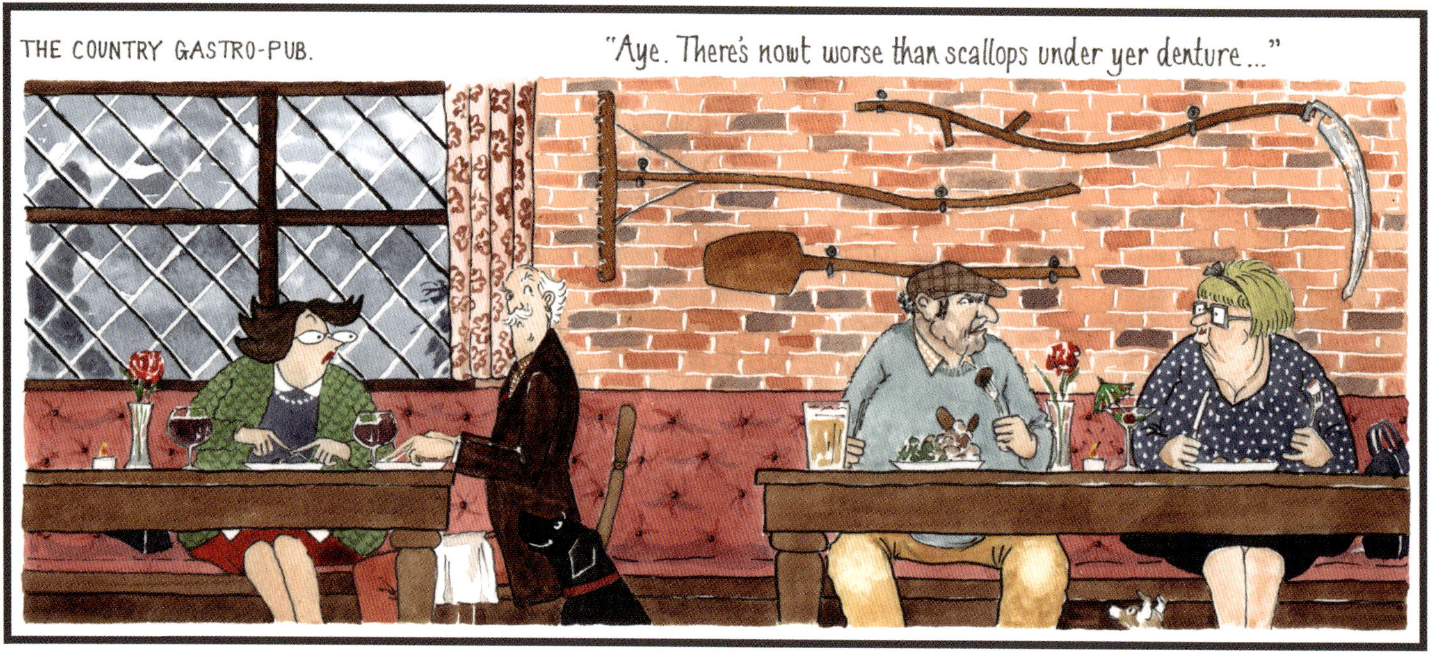
THE COUNTRY GASTRO-PUB.
"Aye. There's nowt worse than scallops under yer denture..."

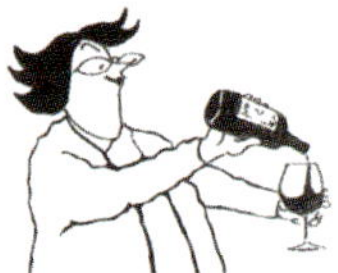

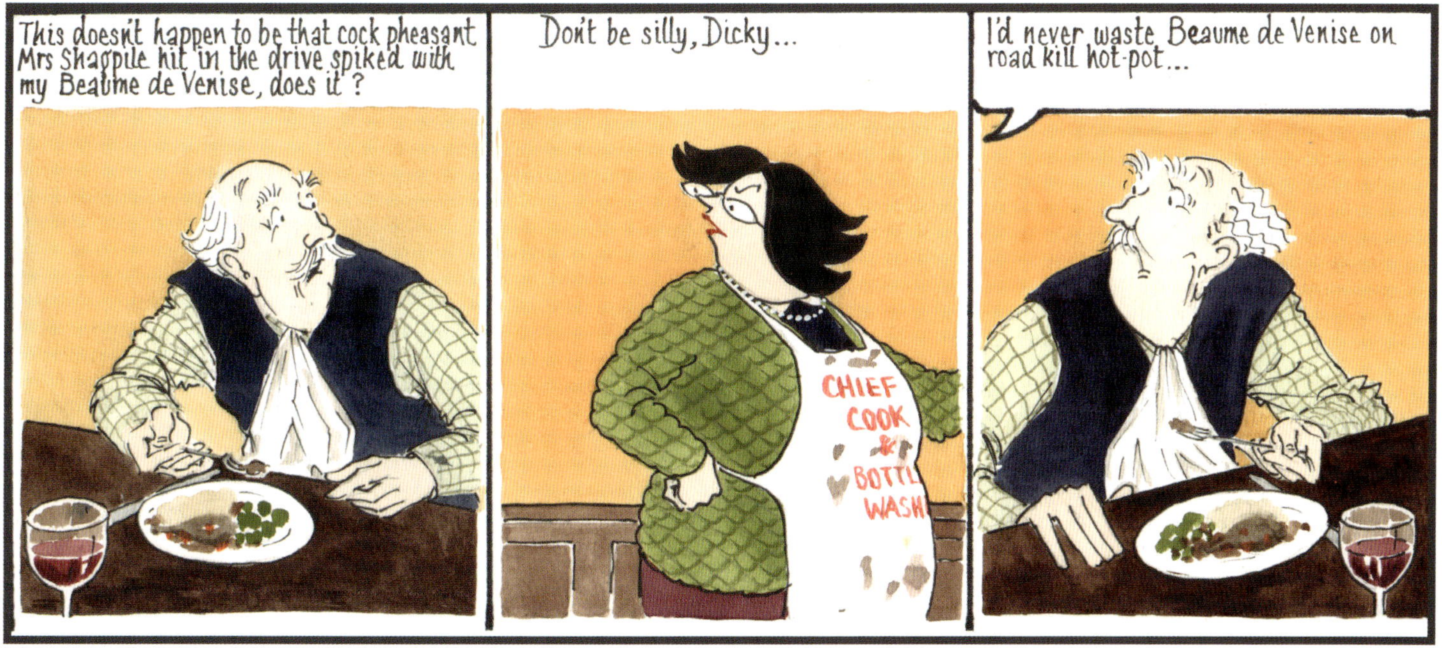
This doesn't happen to be that cock pheasant Mrs Shagpile hit in the drive spiked with my Beaume de Venise, does it?
Don't be silly, Dicky...
CHIEF COOK & BOTTL WASH
I'd never waste Beaume de Venise on road kill hot-pot...

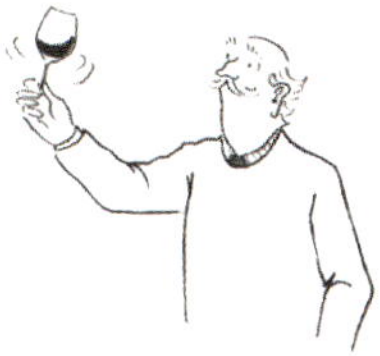

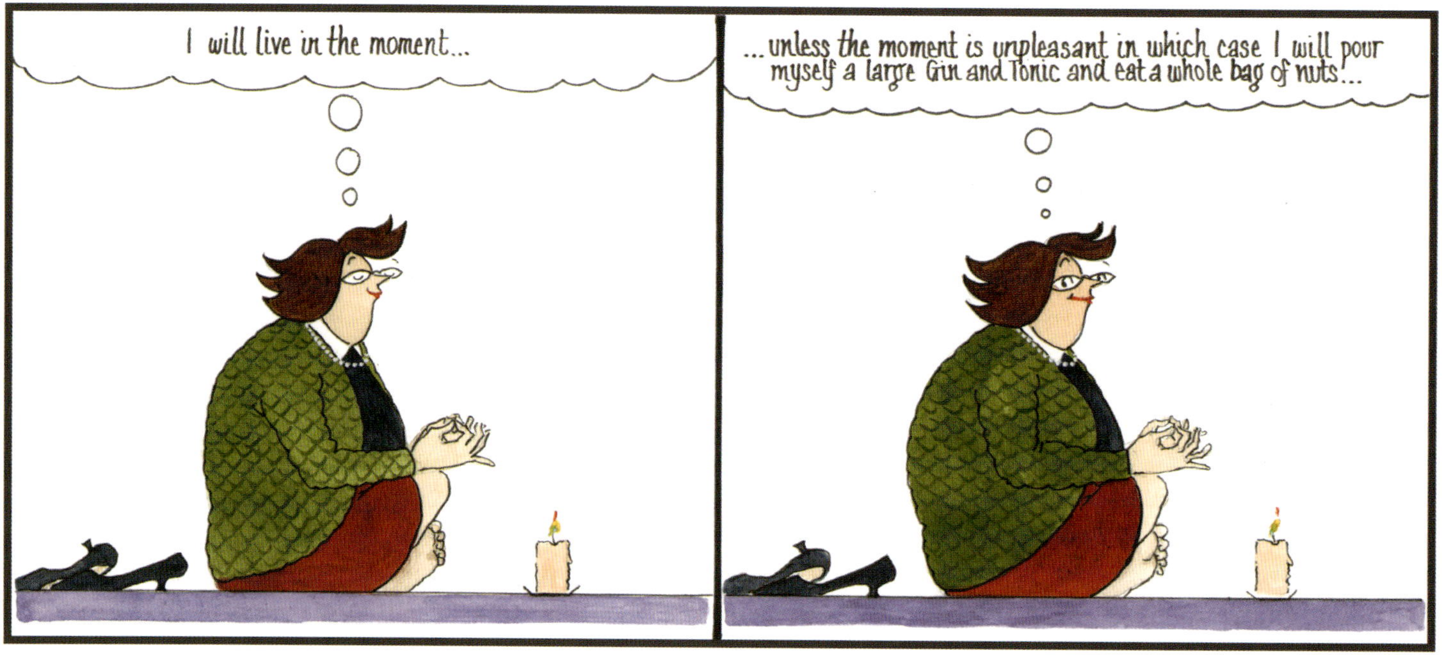
I will live in the moment...
...unless the moment is unpleasant in which case I will pour myself a large Gin and Tonic and eat a whole bag of nuts!...

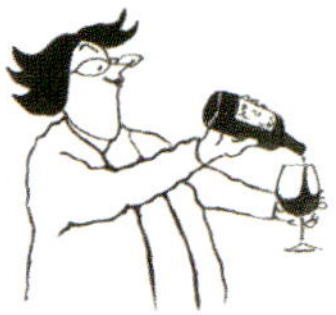

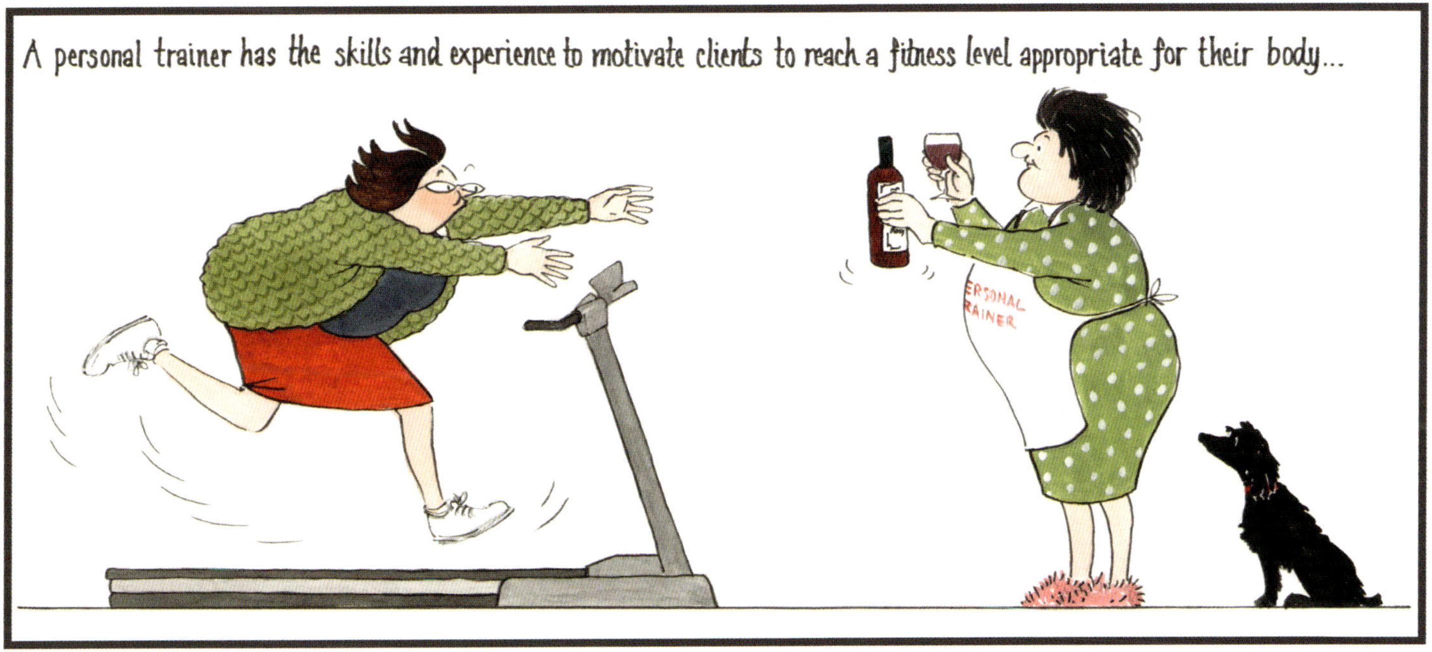
A personal trainer has the skills and experience to motivate clients to reach a fitness level appropriate for their body...
ERSONAL
RAINER

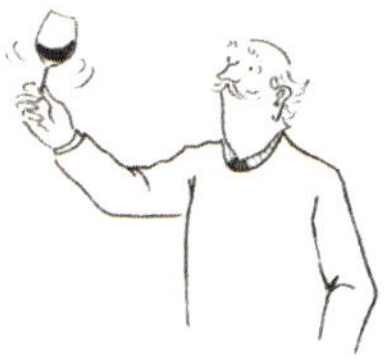

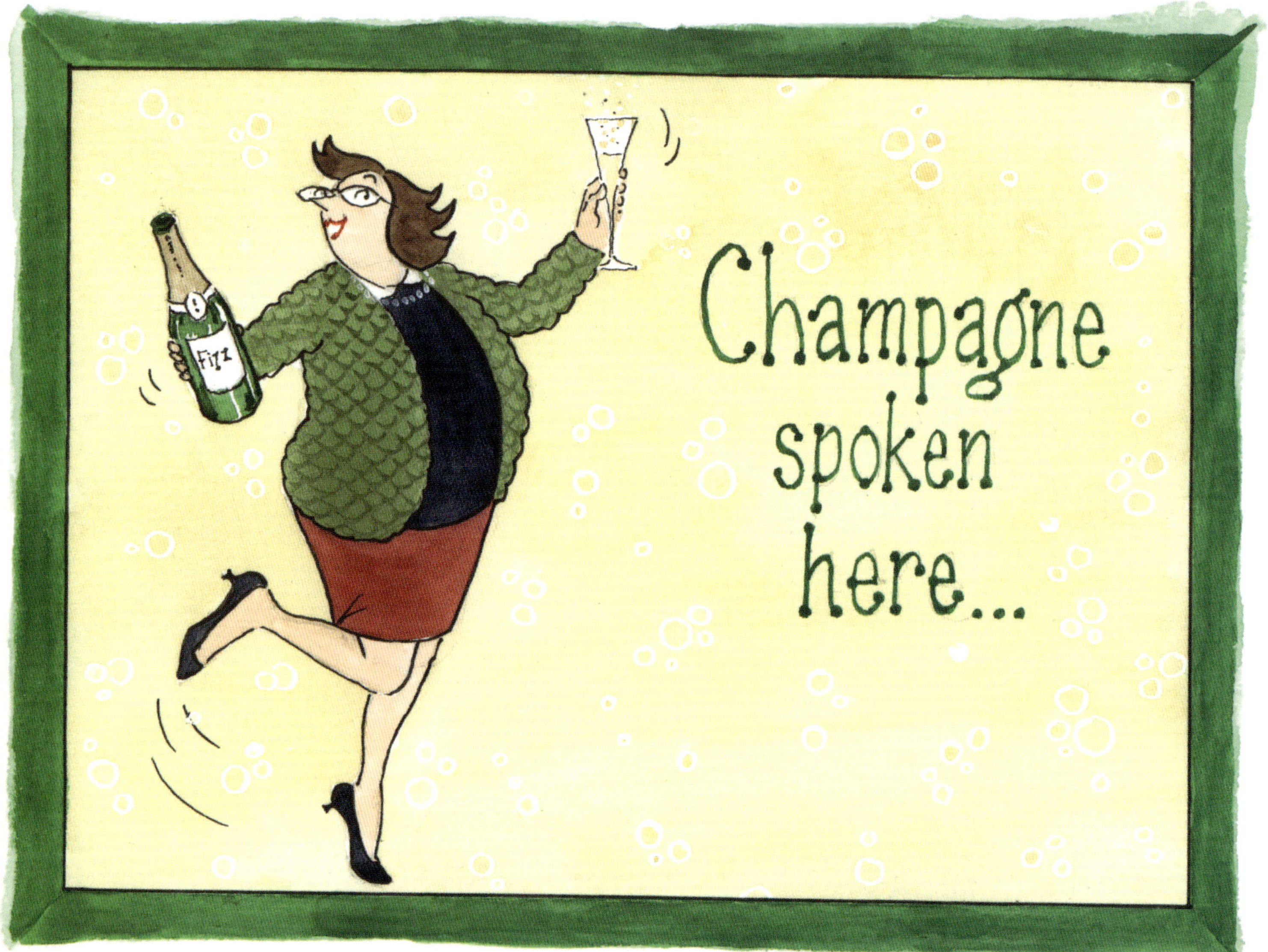
Fizz
Champagne
spoken
here...

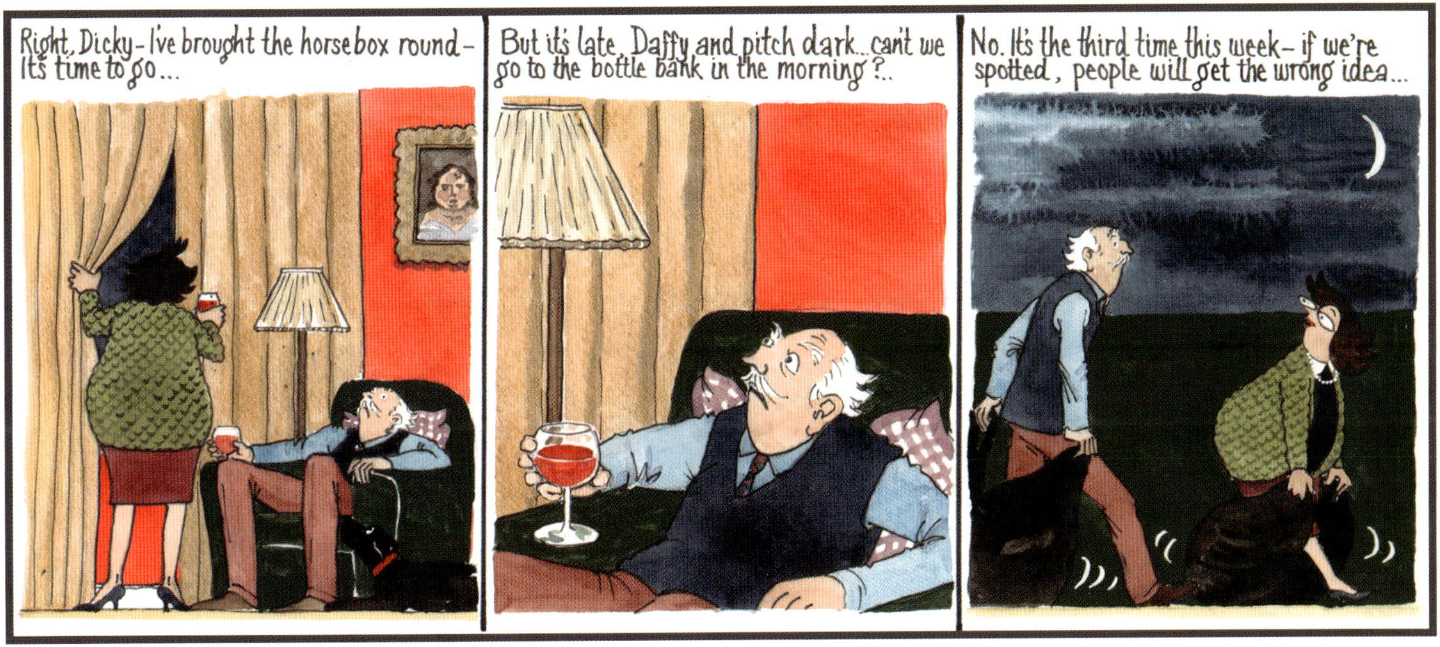
Right, Dicky – I've brought the horsebox round – It's time to go...
But it's late, Daffy and pitch dark... can't we go to the bottle bank in the morning?..
No. It's the third time this week – if we're spotted, people will get the wrong idea...

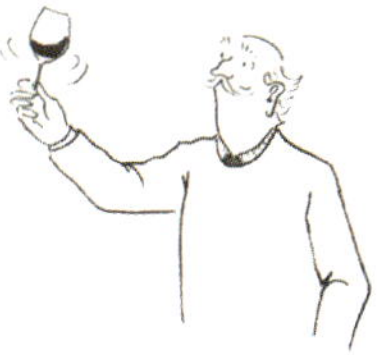

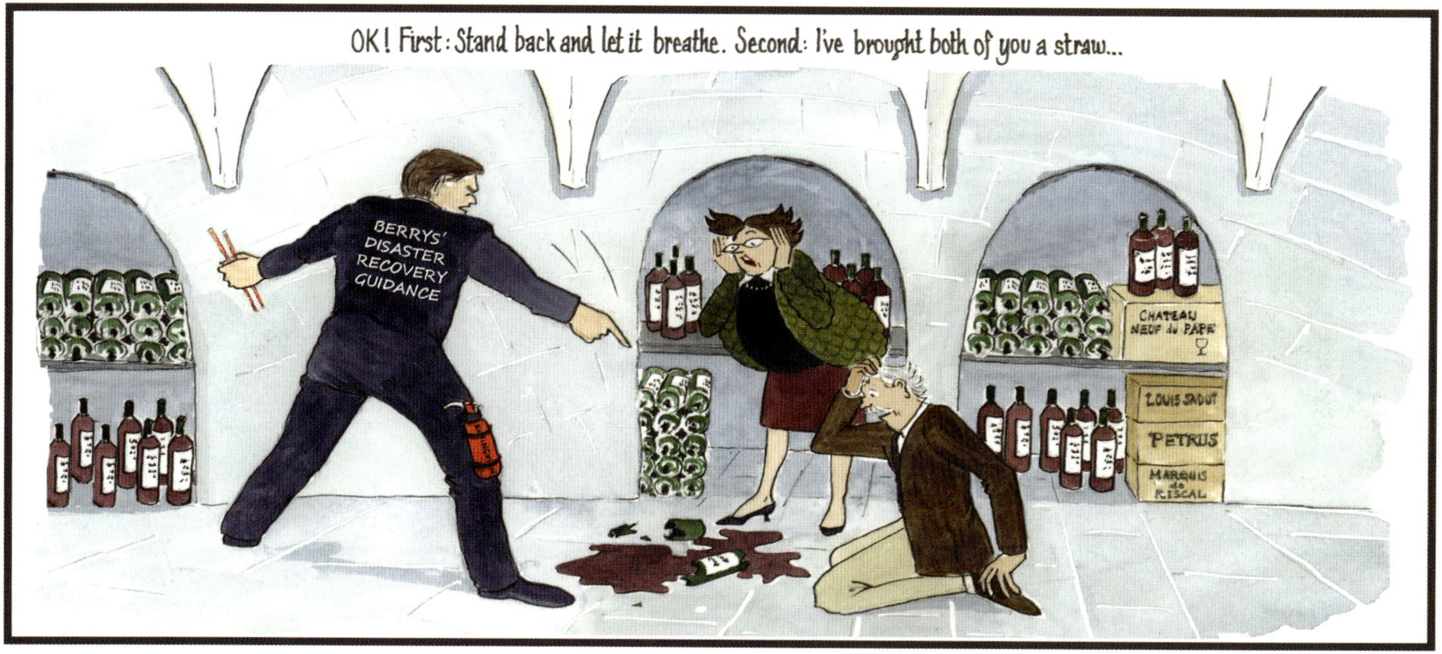
BERRYS' DISASTER RECOVERY GUIDANCE
CHATEAU NEUF du PAPE
PETRUS
MARQUIS de RISCAL

OK! First: Stand back and let it breathe. Second: I've brought both of you a straw...

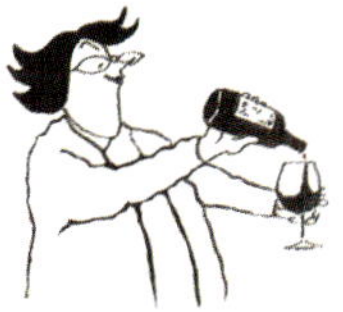

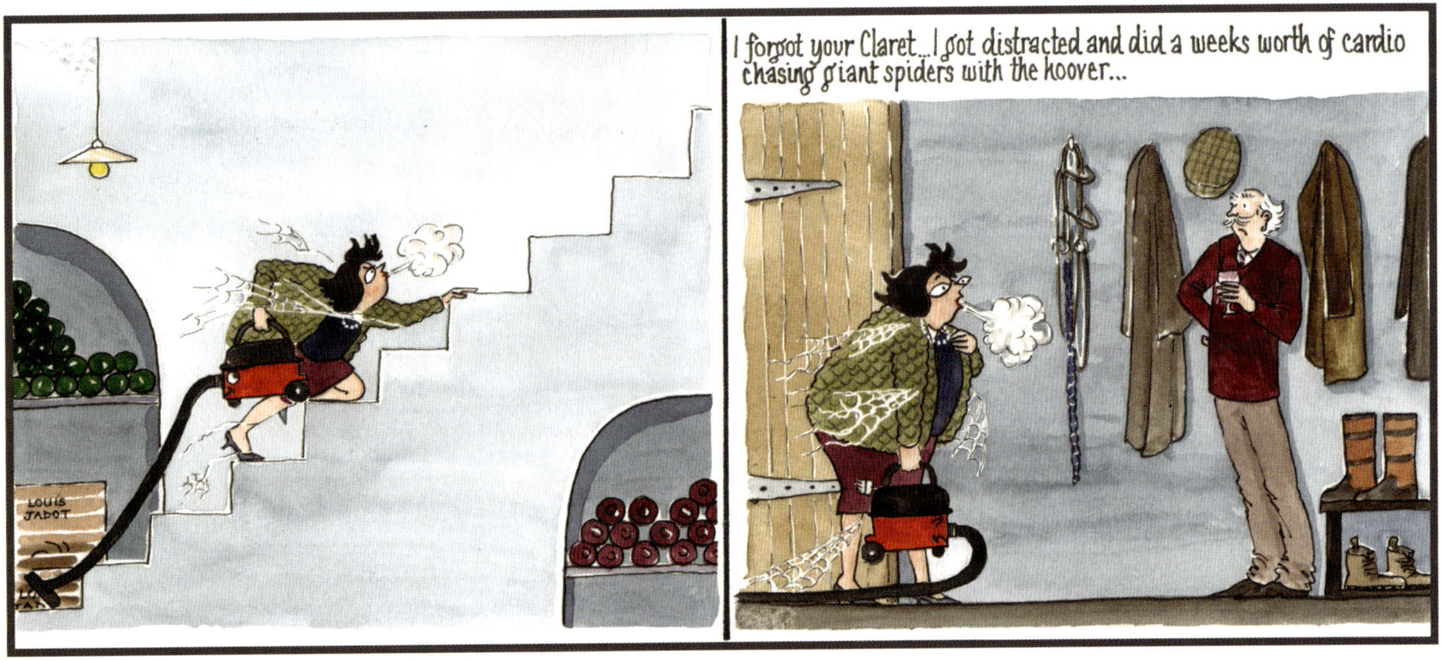
LOUIS
JADOT
I forgot your Claret...I got distracted and did a weeks worth of cardio chasing giant spiders with the hoover...

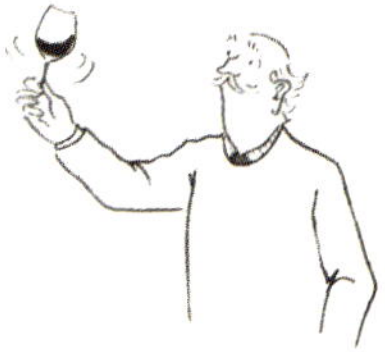

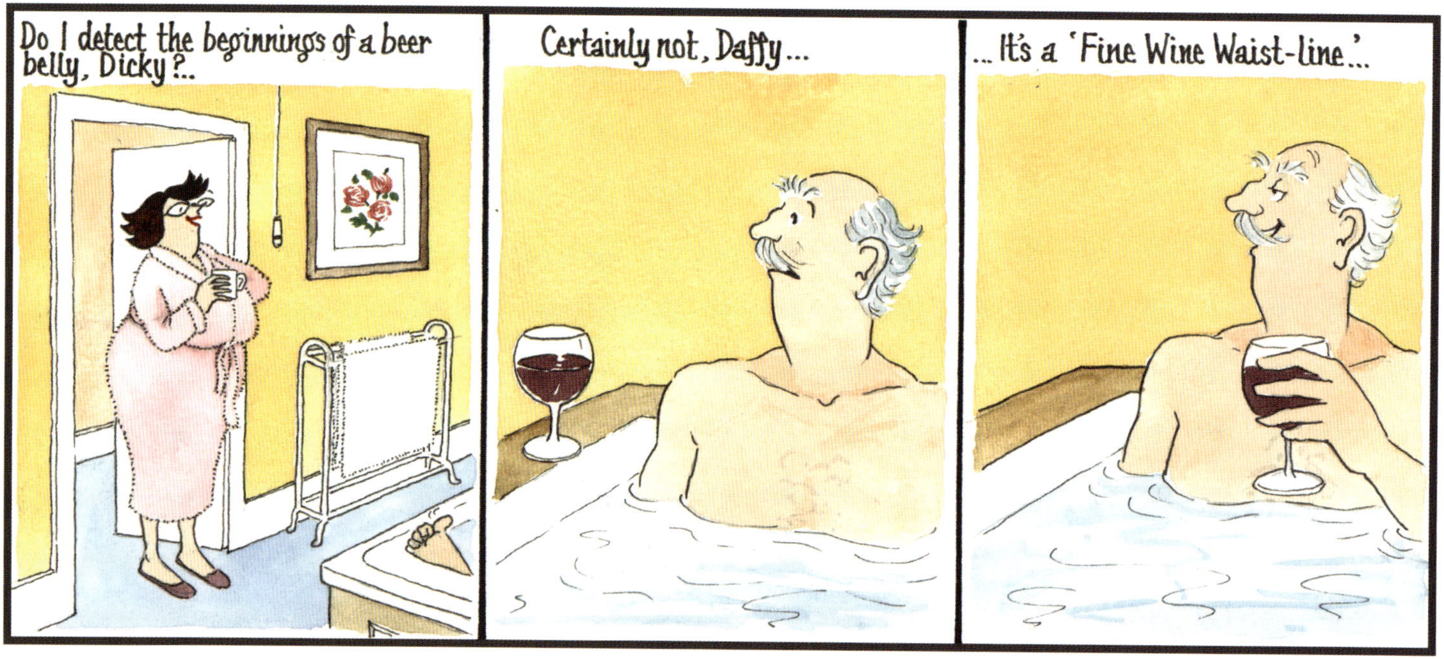
Do I detect the beginnings of a beer belly, Dicky?..
Certainly not, Daffy...
... It's a 'Fine Wine Waist-line.'...

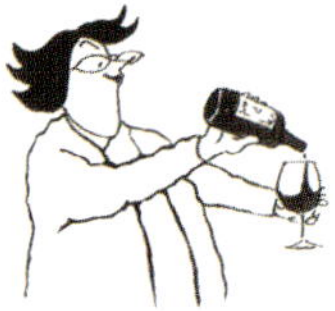

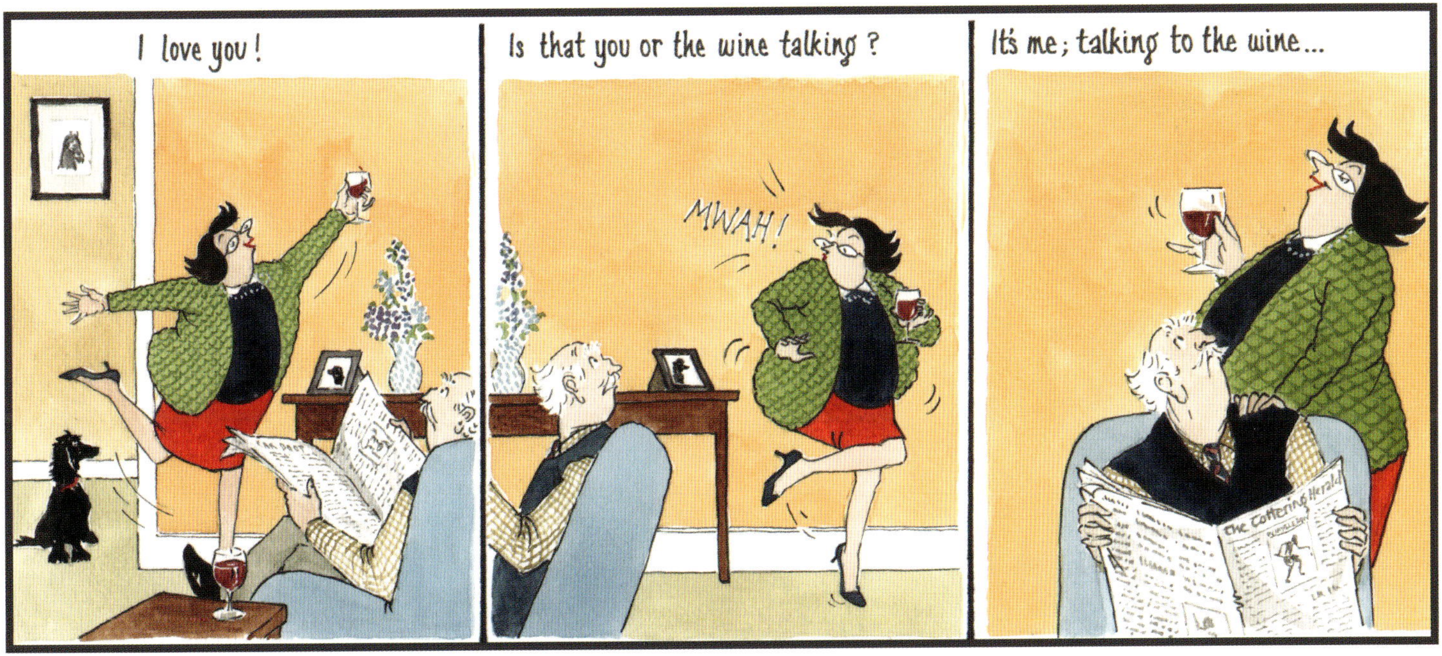
I love you!
Is that you or the wine talking?
MWAH!
It's me; talking to the wine...
The Cottering Herald

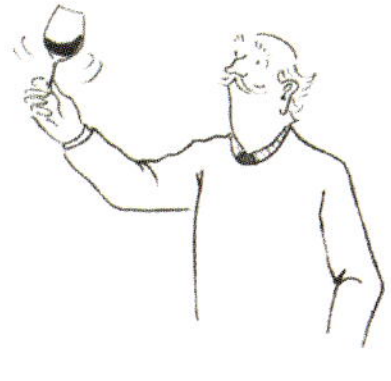

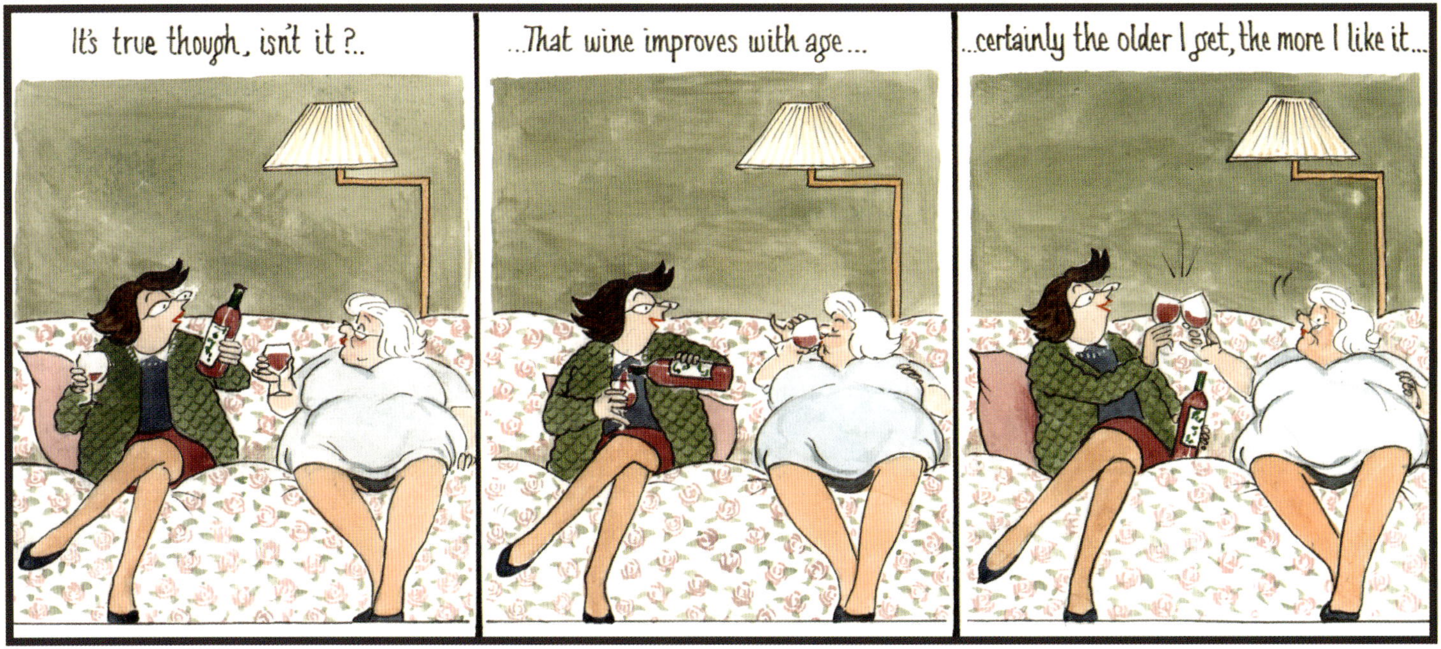
It's true though, isn't it ?..
...That wine improves with age...
...certainly the older I get, the more I like it...

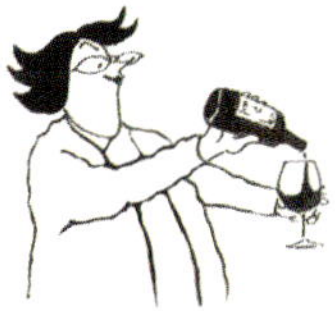

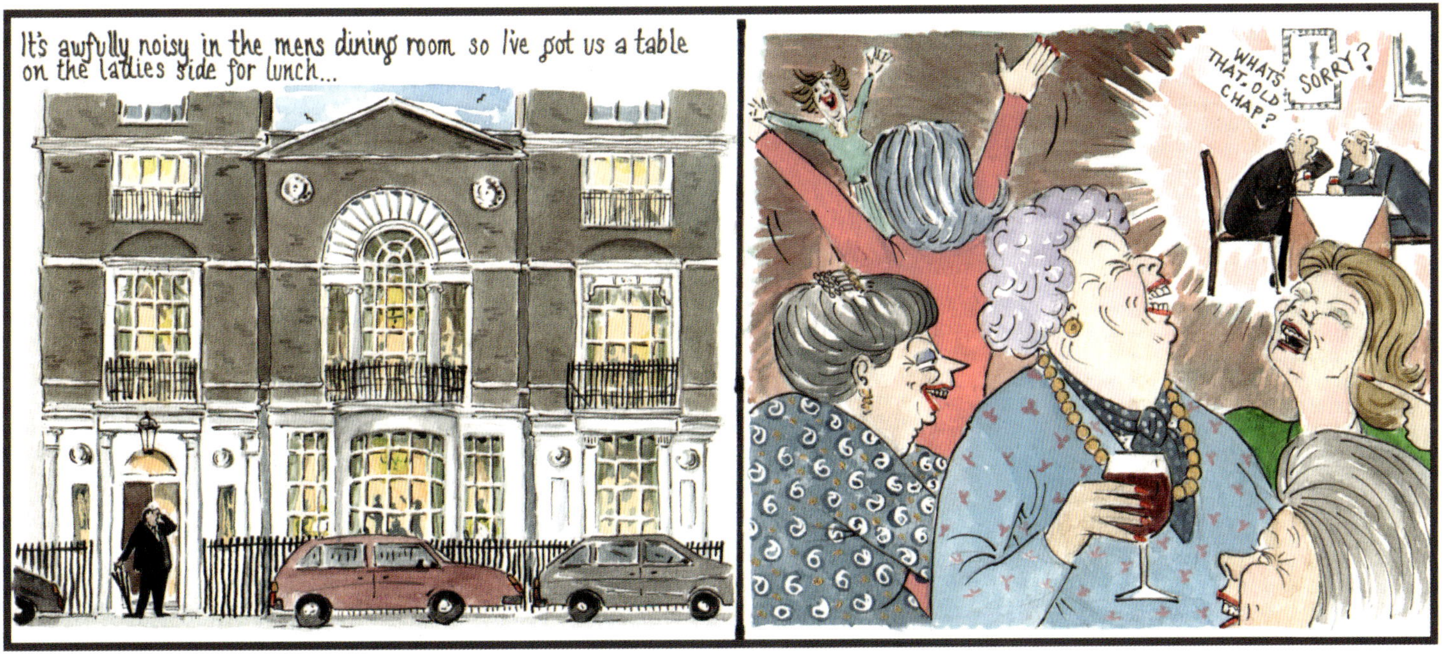
It's awfully noisy in the mens dining room so I've got us a table on the ladies side for lunch...
WHATS THAT, OLD CHAP?
SORRY?

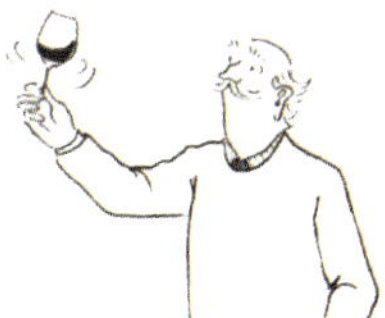

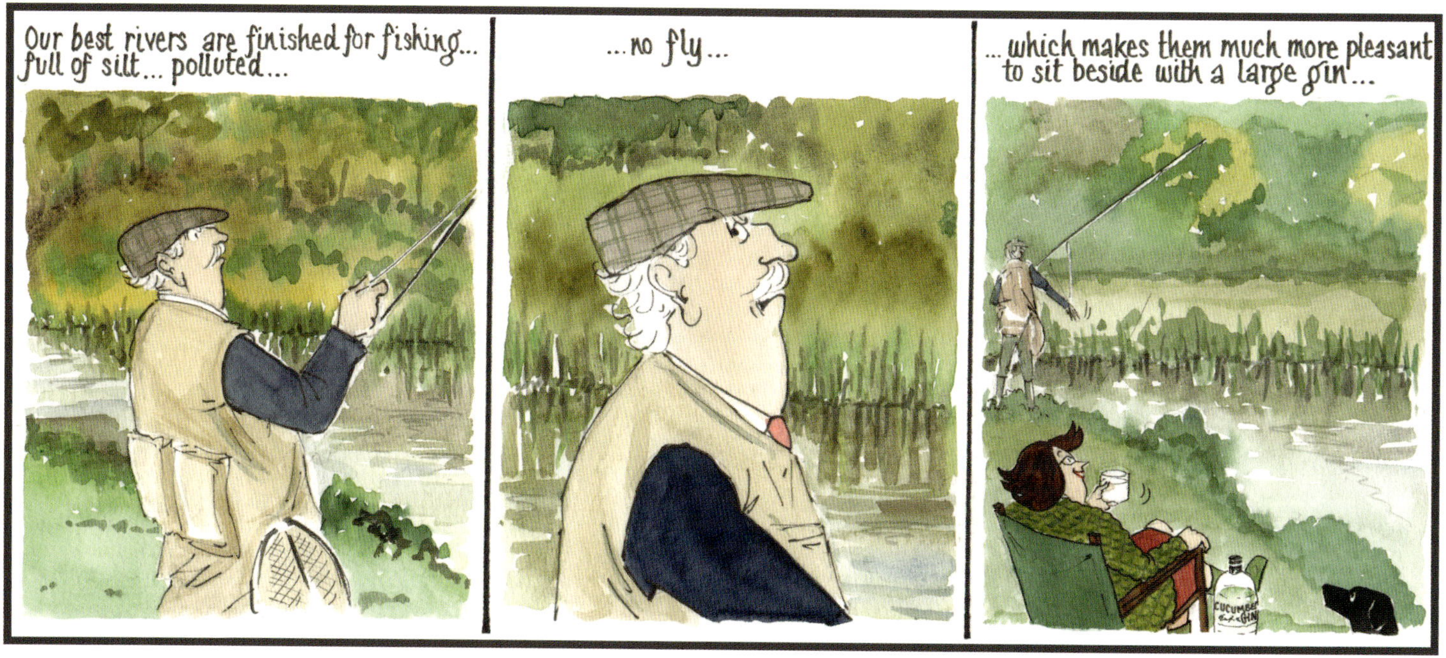
Our best rivers are finished for fishing... full of silt... polluted...
...no fly...
...which makes them much more pleasant to sit beside with a large gin...

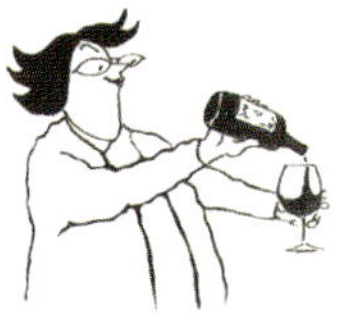

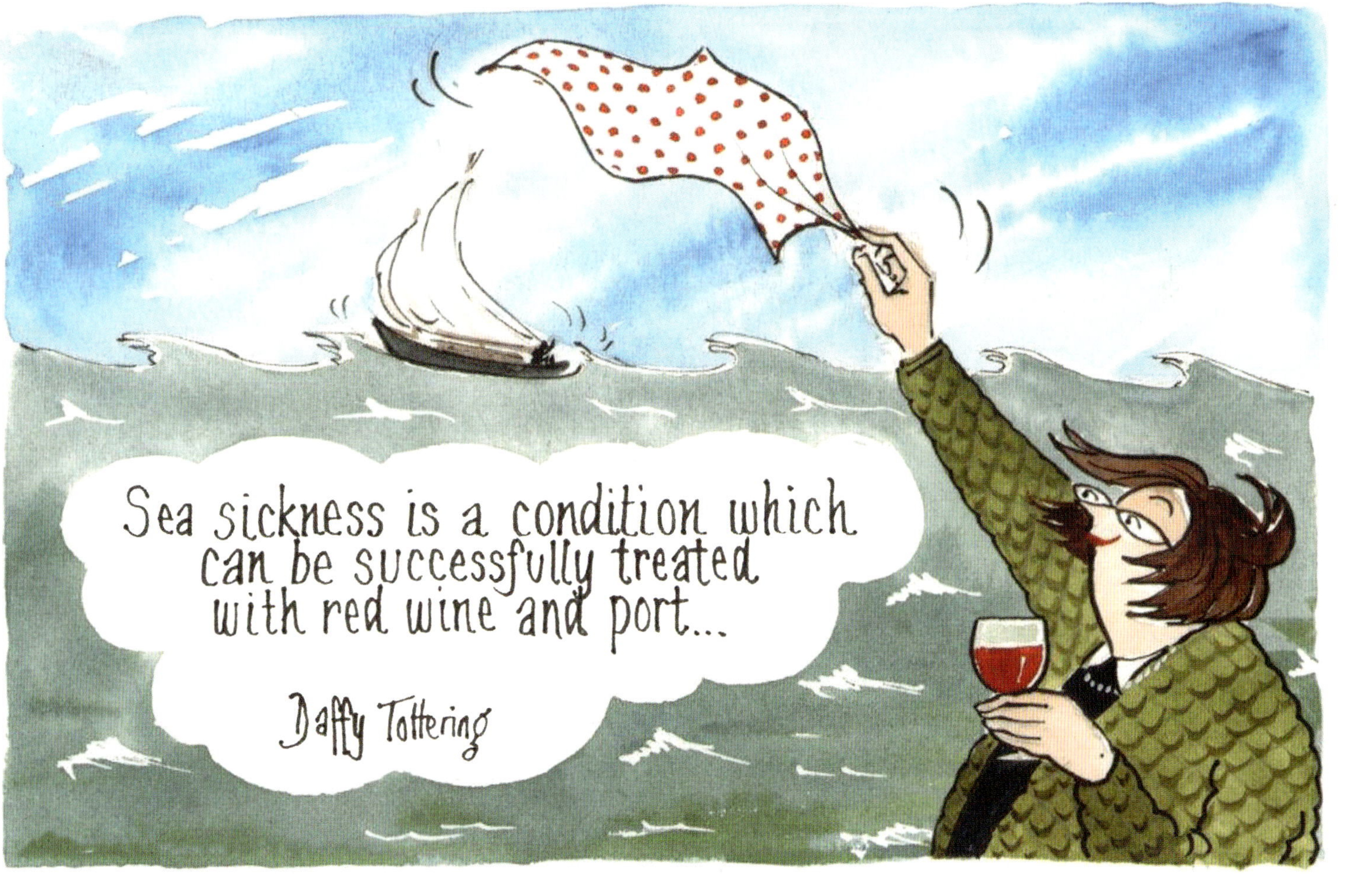
Sea sickness is a condition which can be successfully treated with red wine and port...
Daffy Tottering

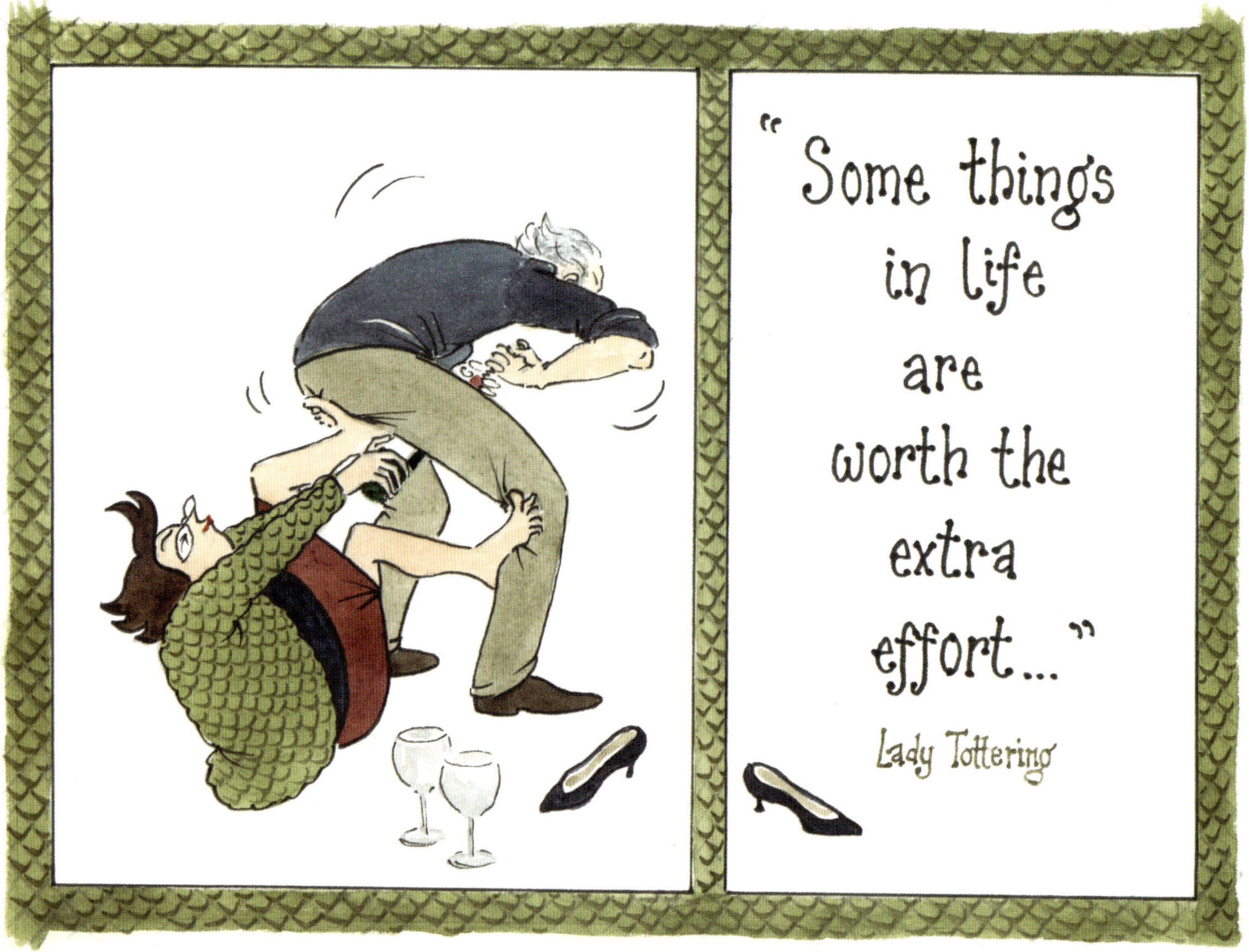
"Some things in life are worth the extra effort..."
Lady Tottering

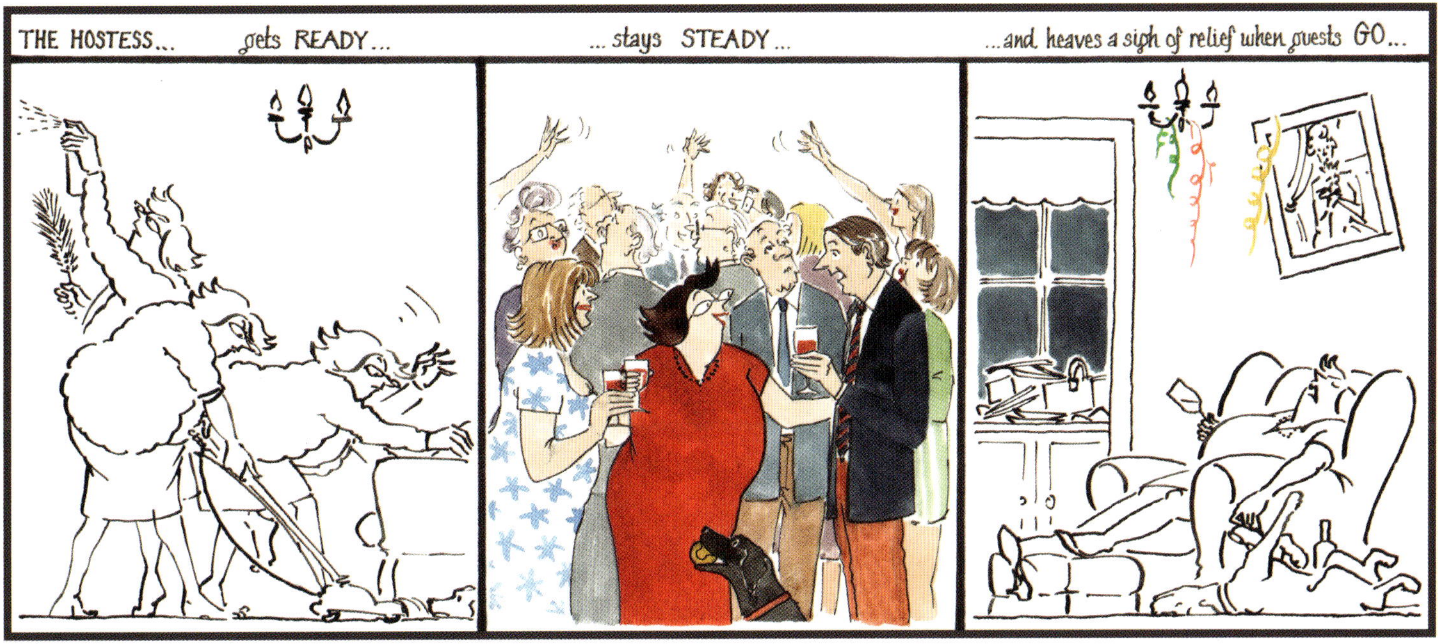
THE HOSTESS... gets READY...
... stays STEADY...
...and heaves a sigh of relief when guests GO...

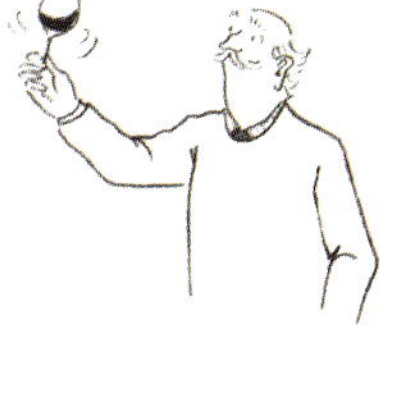

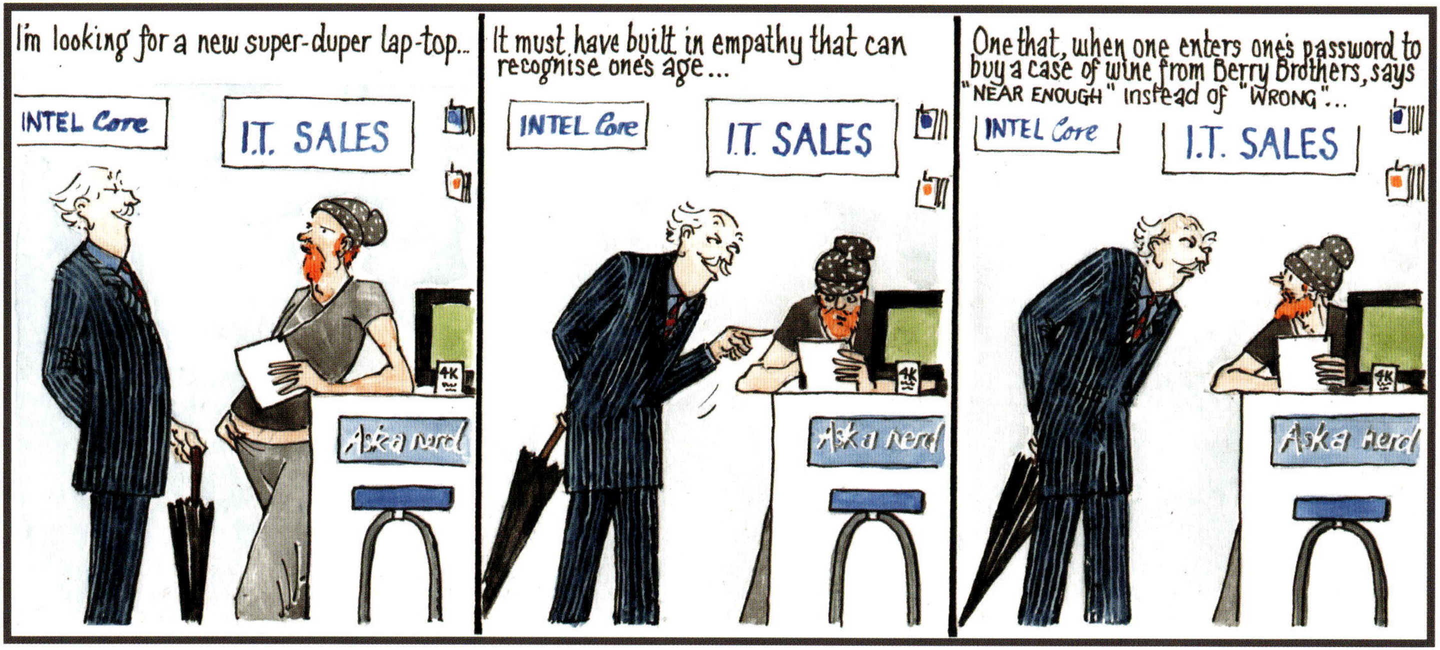
I'm looking for a new super-duper lap-top...
INTEL Core
I.T. SALES
Ask a nerd
It must have built in empathy that can recognise one's age...
INTEL Core
I.T. SALES
Ask a nerd
One that, when one enters one's password to buy a case of wine from Berry Brothers, says "NEAR ENOUGH" instead of "WRONG"...
INTEL Core
I.T. SALES
Ask a nerd

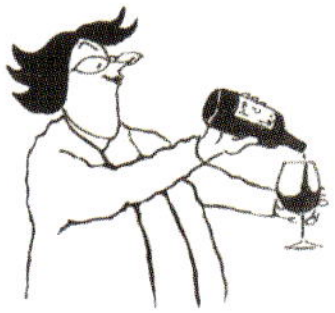

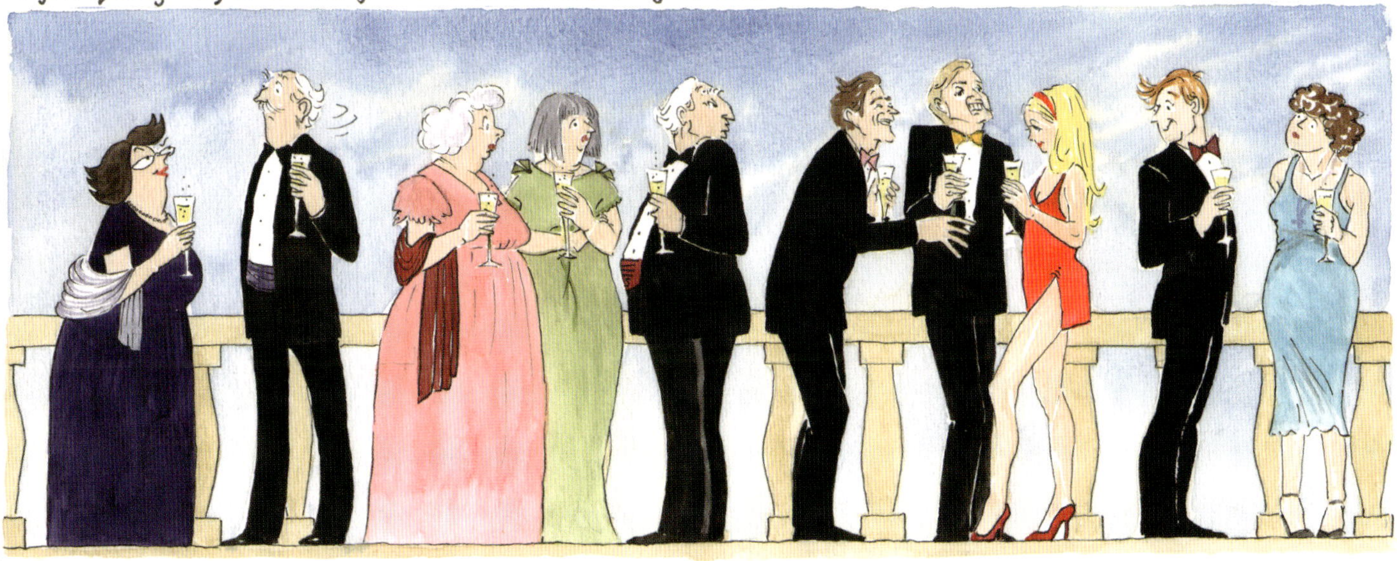

I feel quietly confident that if I wore that dress, everyone would look at me, too...

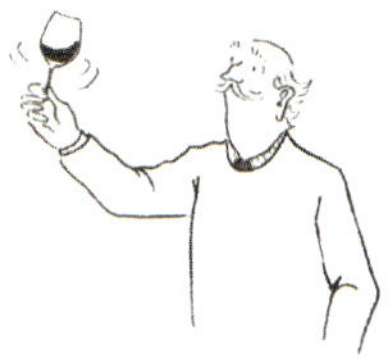

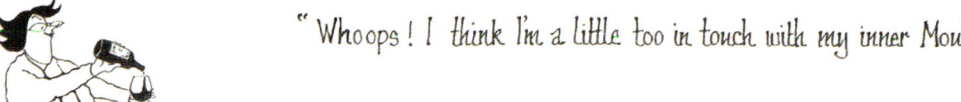
"Whoops! I think I'm a little too in touch with my inner Mouton Roths-child…"

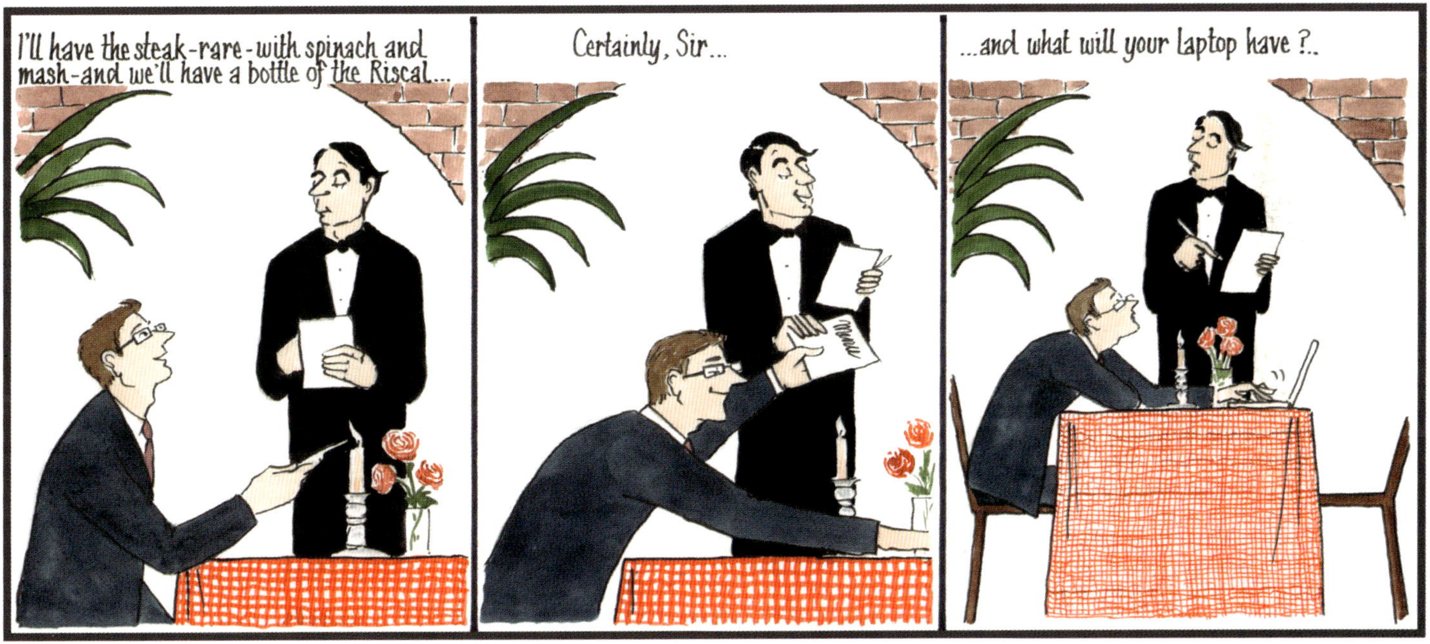
I'll have the steak-rare-with spinach and mash-and we'll have a bottle of the Riscal...
Certainly, Sir...
Menu
...and what will your laptop have ?..

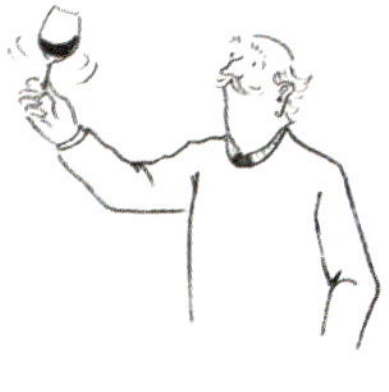

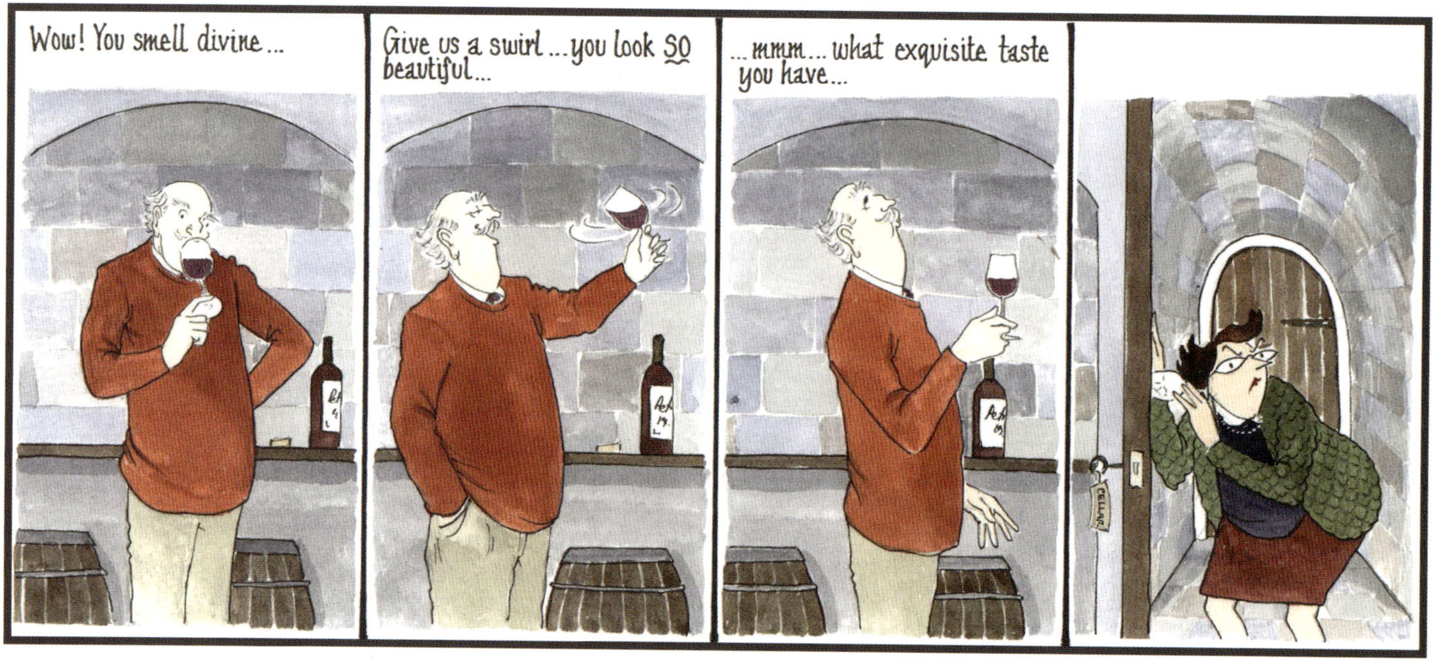
Wow! You smell divine...
Give us a swirl ...you look SO beautiful...
...mmm... what exquisite taste you have...
CELLAR

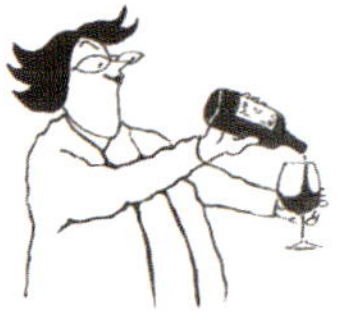

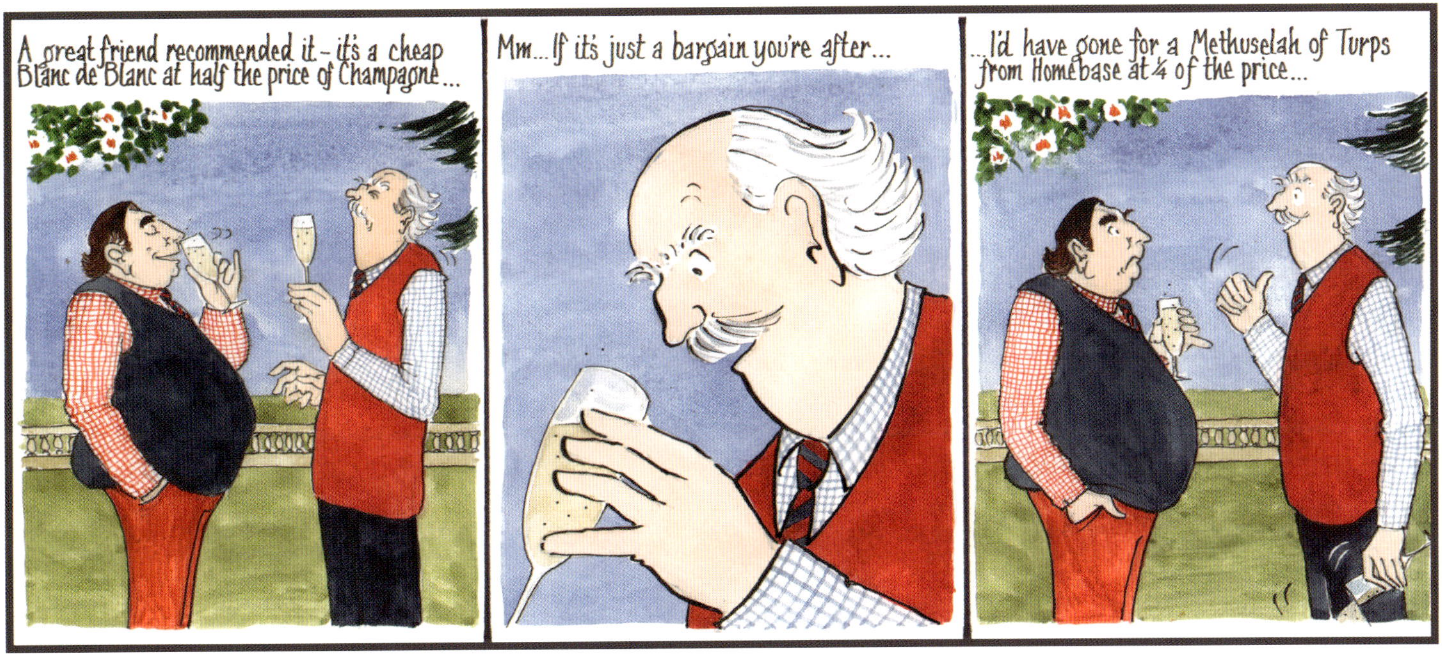
A great friend recommended it – it's a cheap Blanc de Blanc at half the price of Champagne...
Mm... If it's just a bargain you're after...
...I'd have gone for a Methuselah of Turps from Homebase at ¼ of the price...

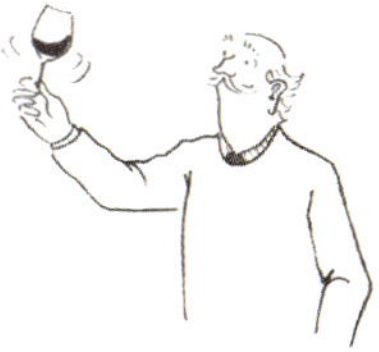

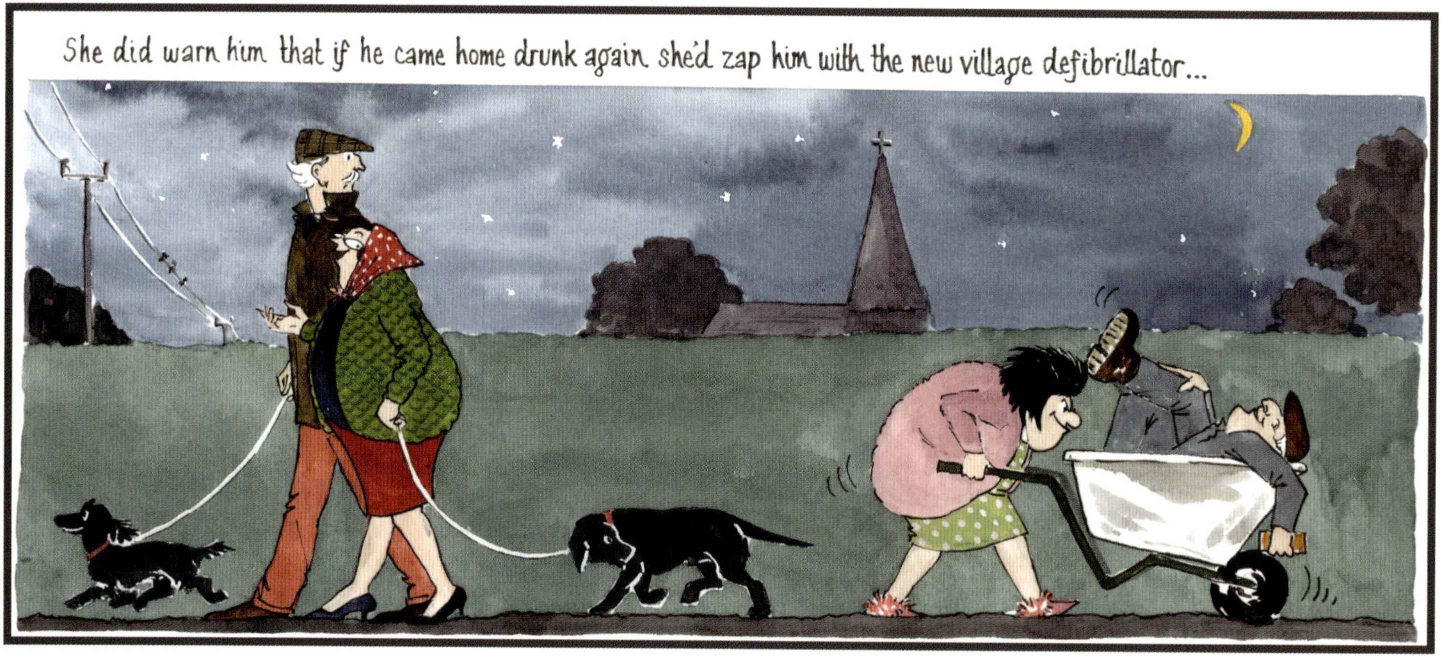
She did warn him that if he came home drunk again she'd zap him with the new village defibrillator...

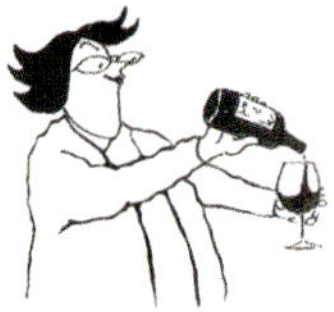

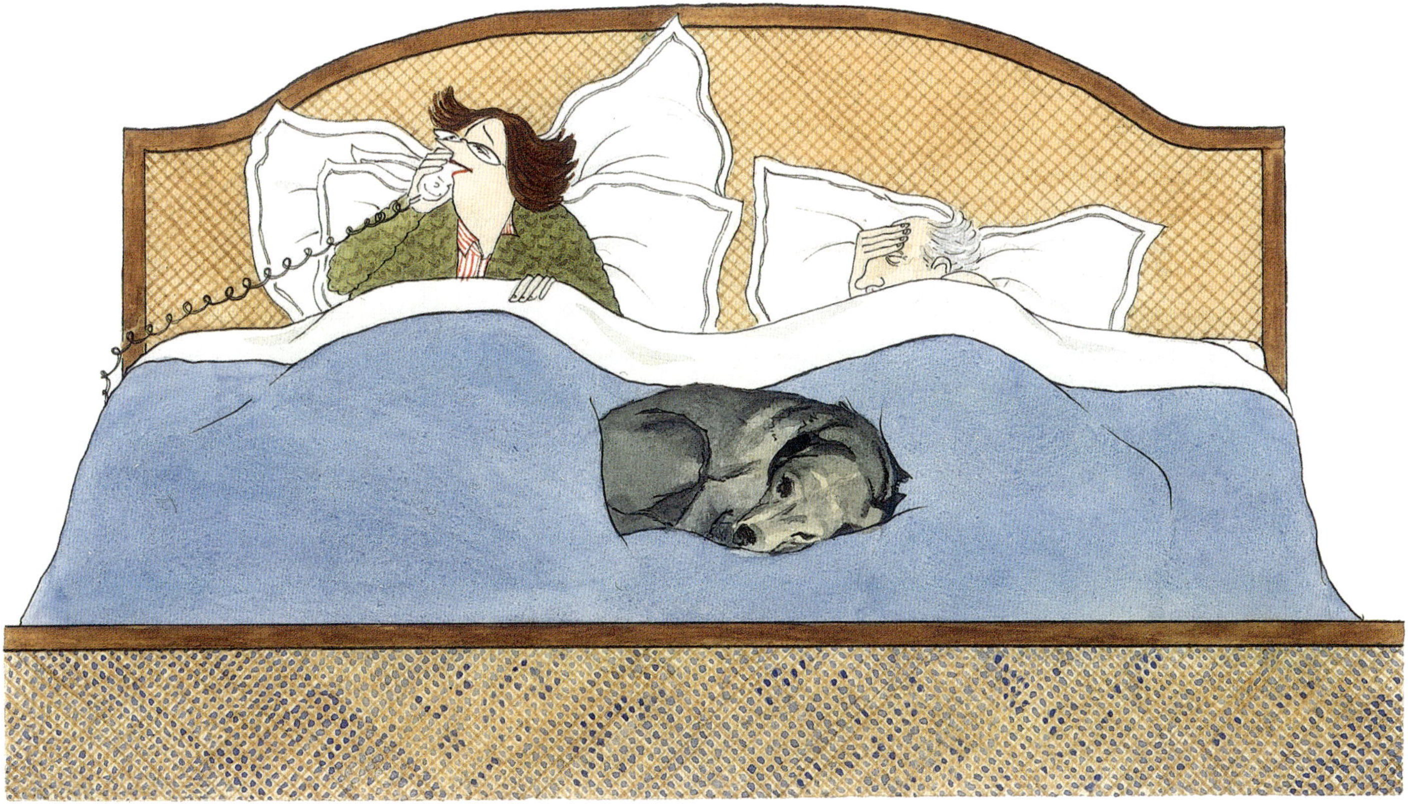

" Emergency services? Two large Bloody Mary's, please..."

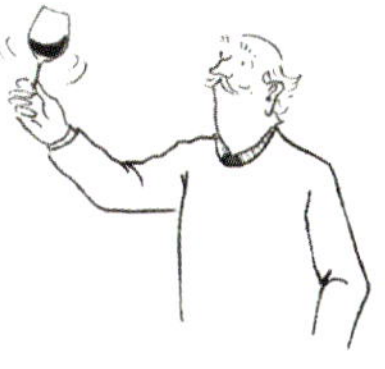

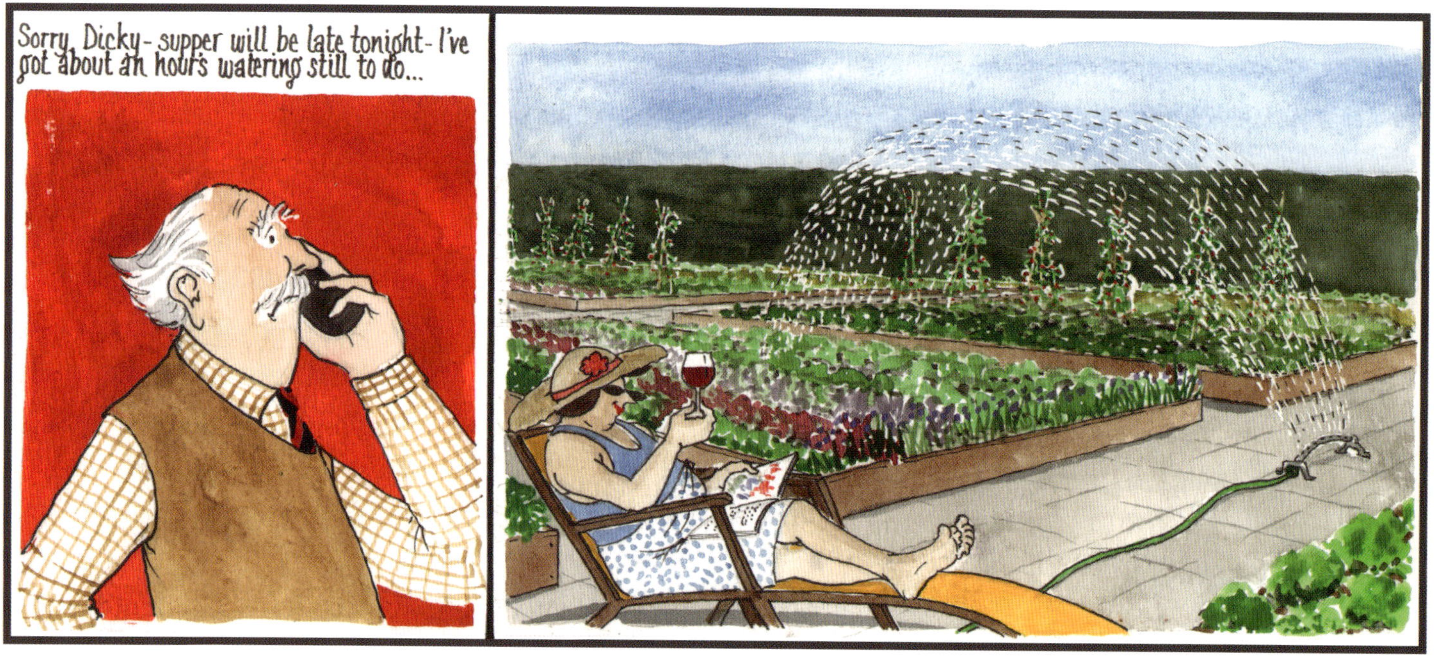
Sorry, Dicky- supper will be late tonight- I've got about an hour's watering still to do...

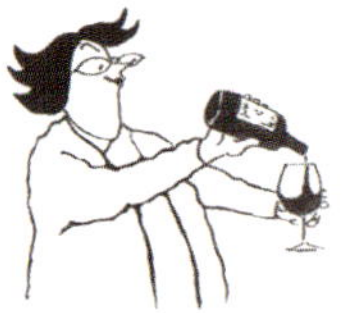

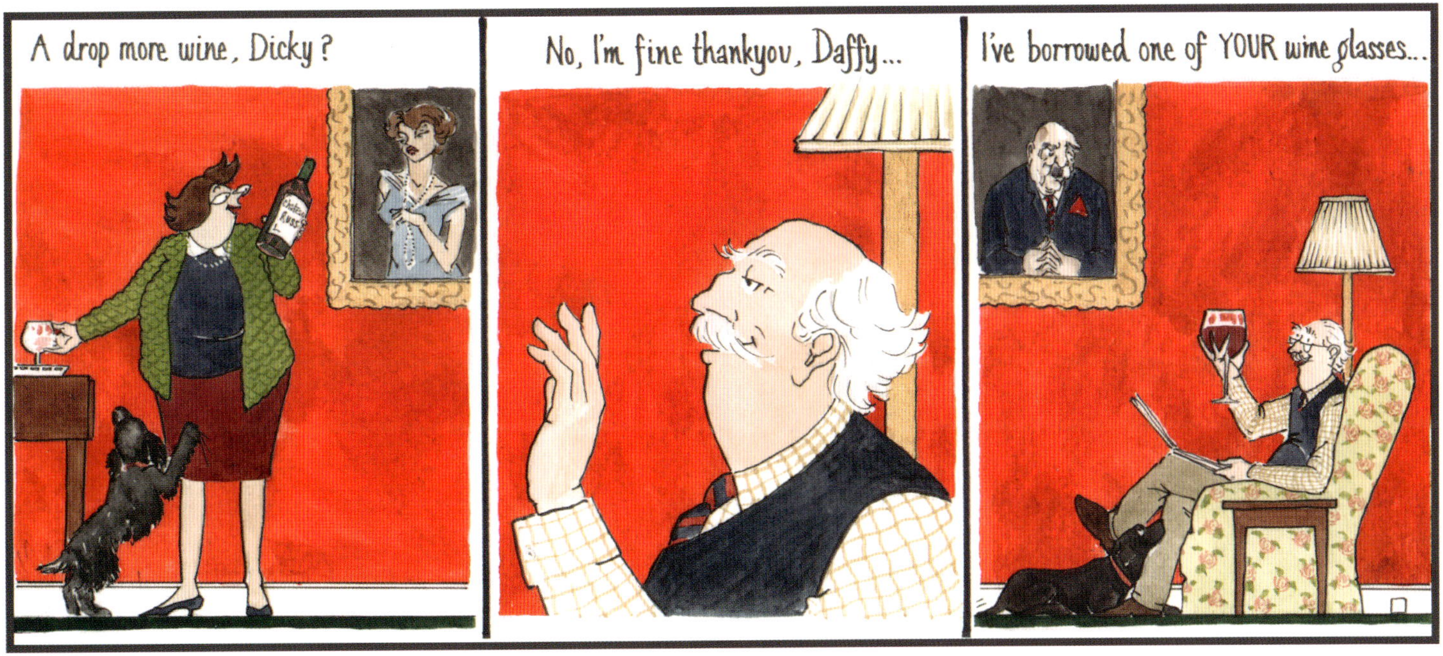
A drop more wine, Dicky?
No, I'm fine thankyou, Daffy...
I've borrowed one of YOUR wine glasses...

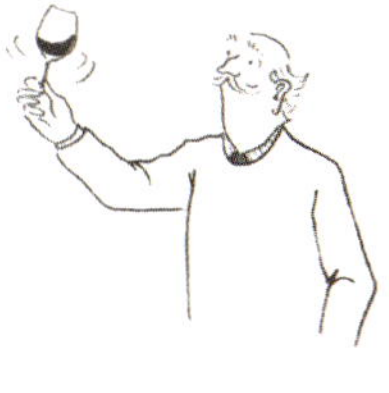

YOUNG AT HEART

...rather more mature in the liver...

...slightly older in other places...

"... The future's not what it
used to be, Dicky ..."

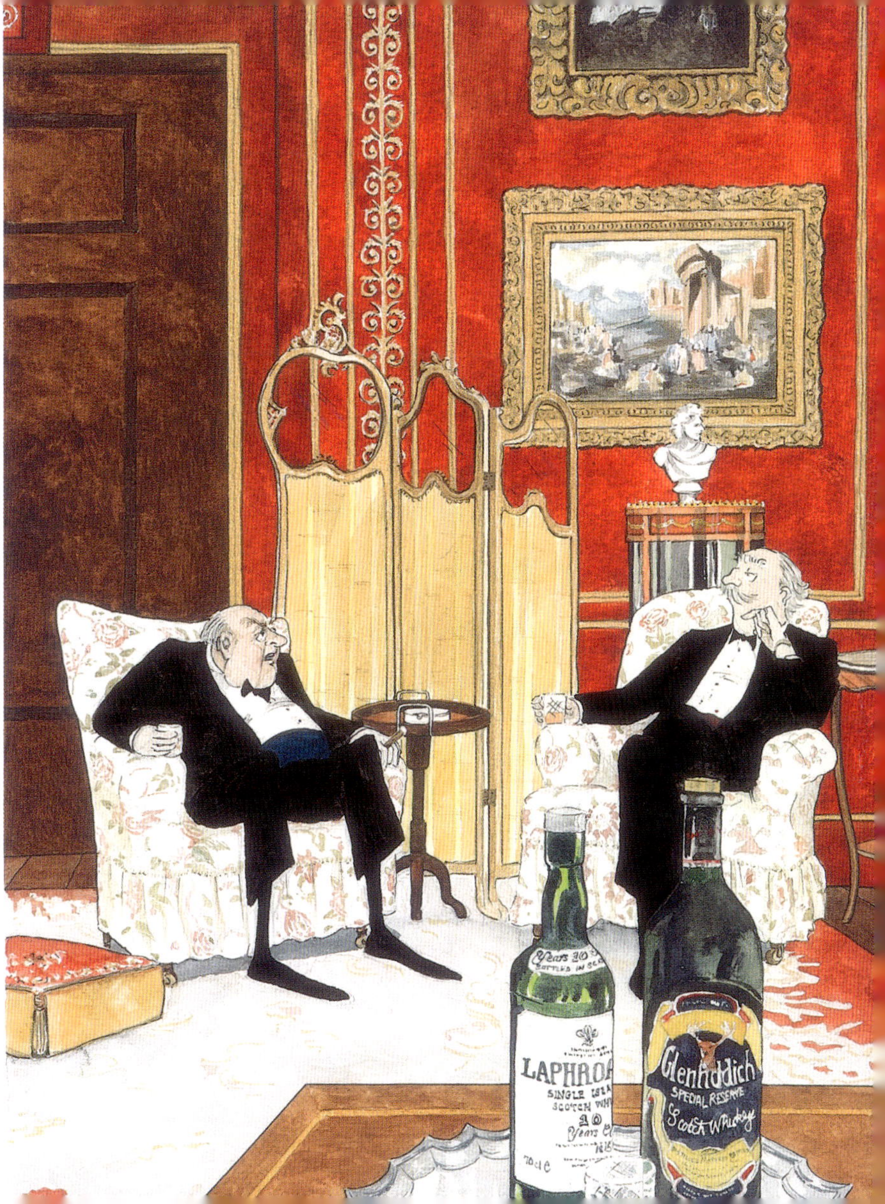
Glenfiddich
SPECIAL RESERVE

Heading for the best spot in the garden for a family sun-downer...

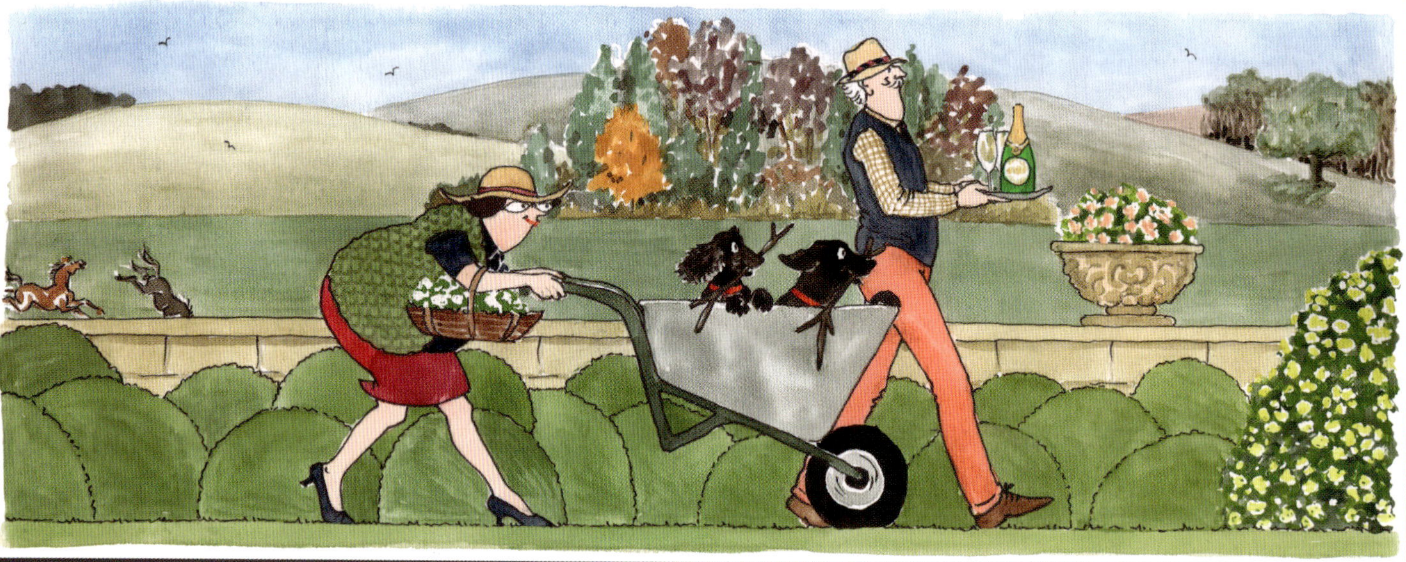

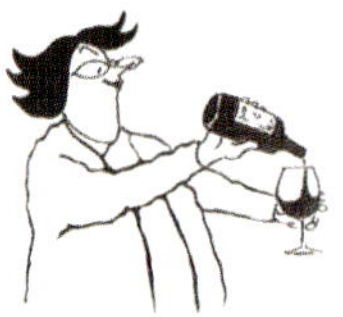

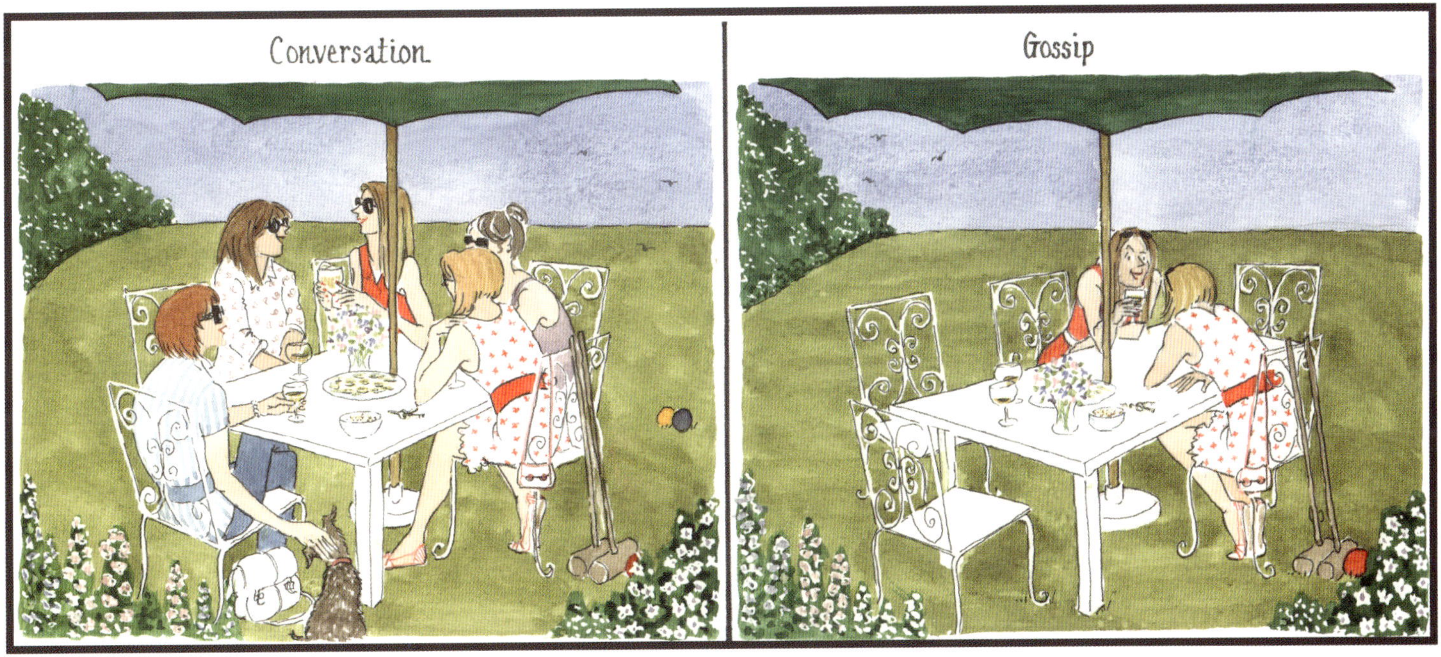
Conversation
Gossip

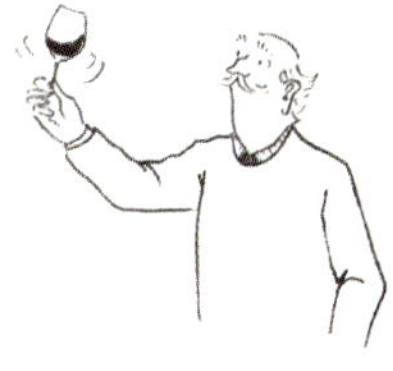

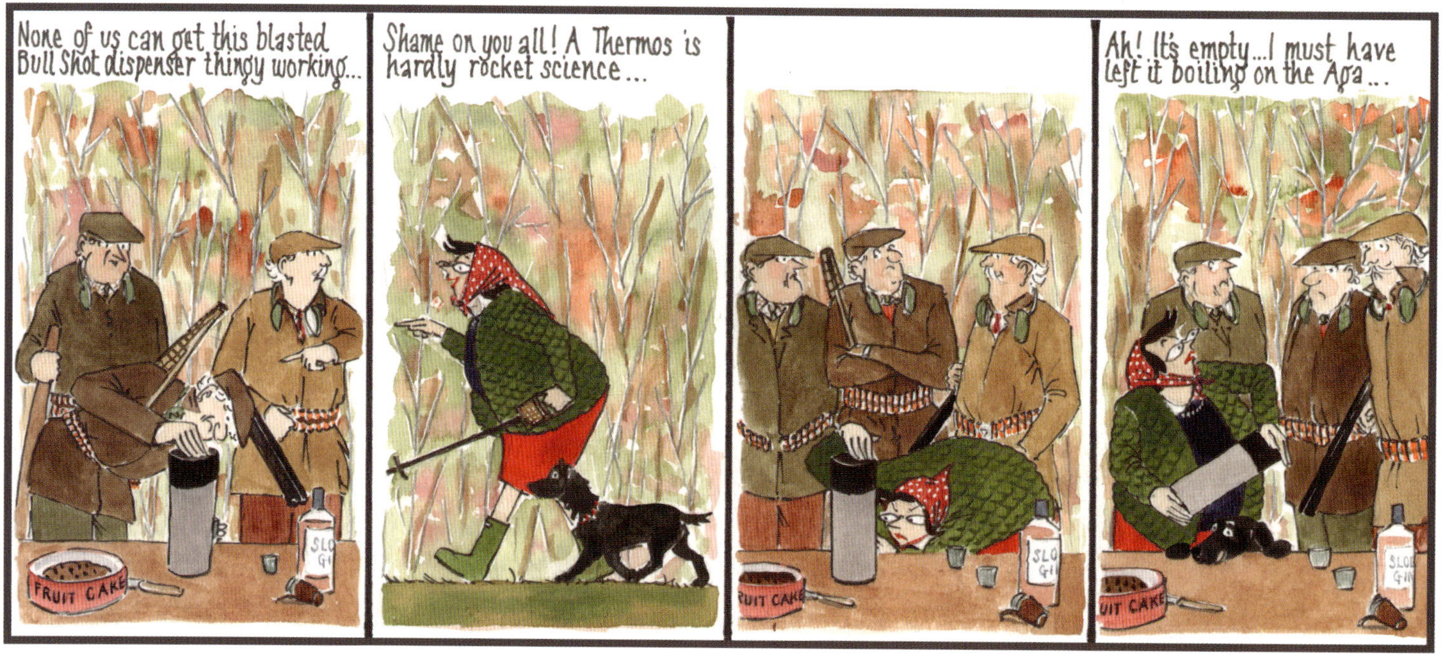
None of us can get this blasted Bull Shot dispenser thingy working...
FRUIT CAKE
Shame on you all! A Thermos is hardly rocket science...
Ah! It's empty...I must have left it boiling on the Aga...

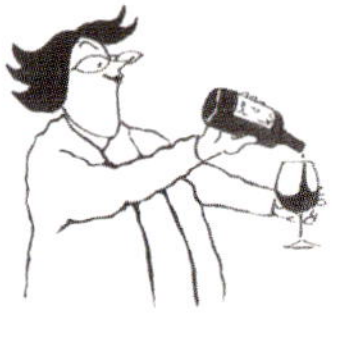

THE ARMED COCKTAIL PARTY...

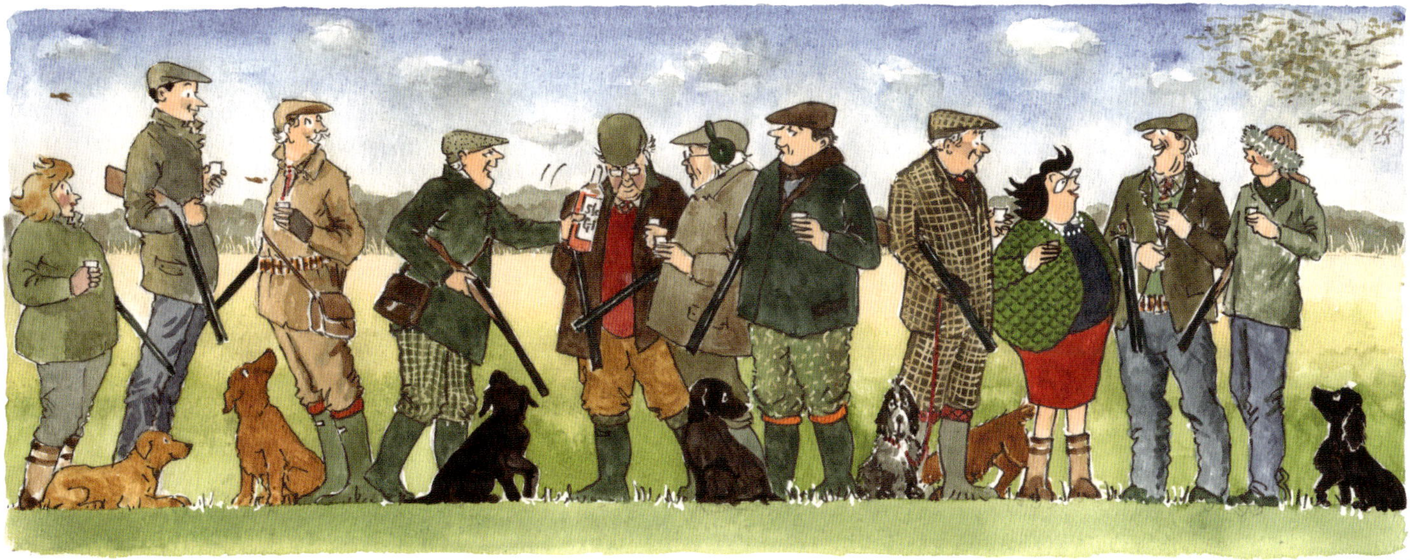

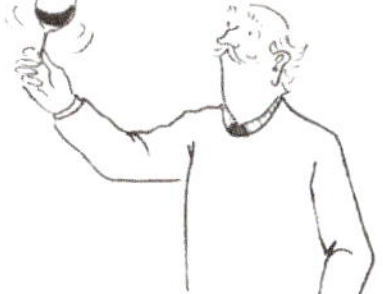

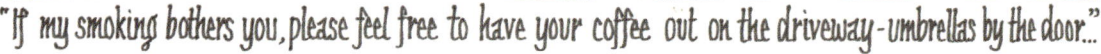

"If my smoking bothers you, please feel free to have your coffee out on the driveway - umbrellas by the door..."

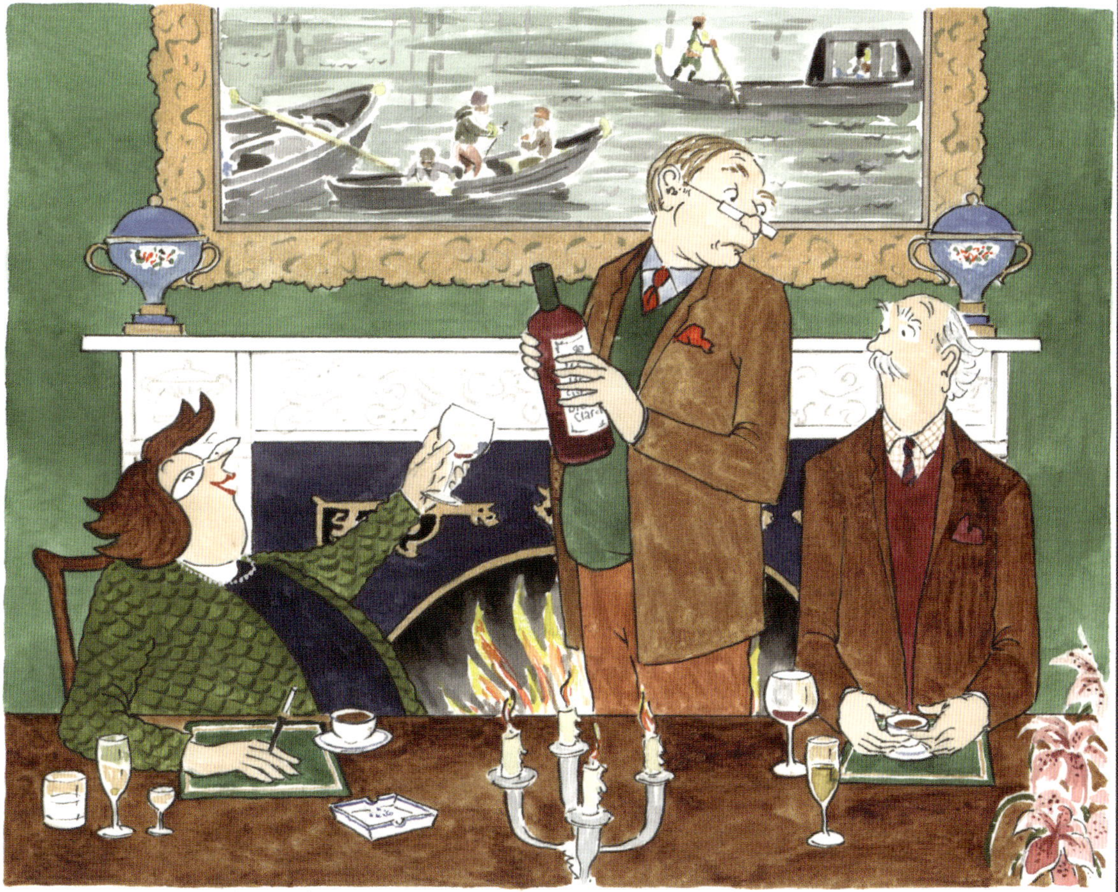

A drop more red wine for me but no more for my husband, thankyou – his face is going all blurry…

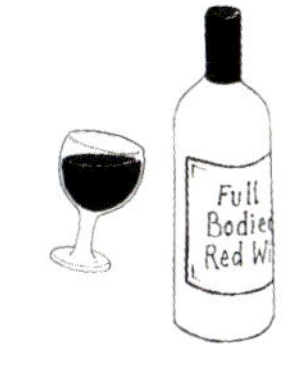

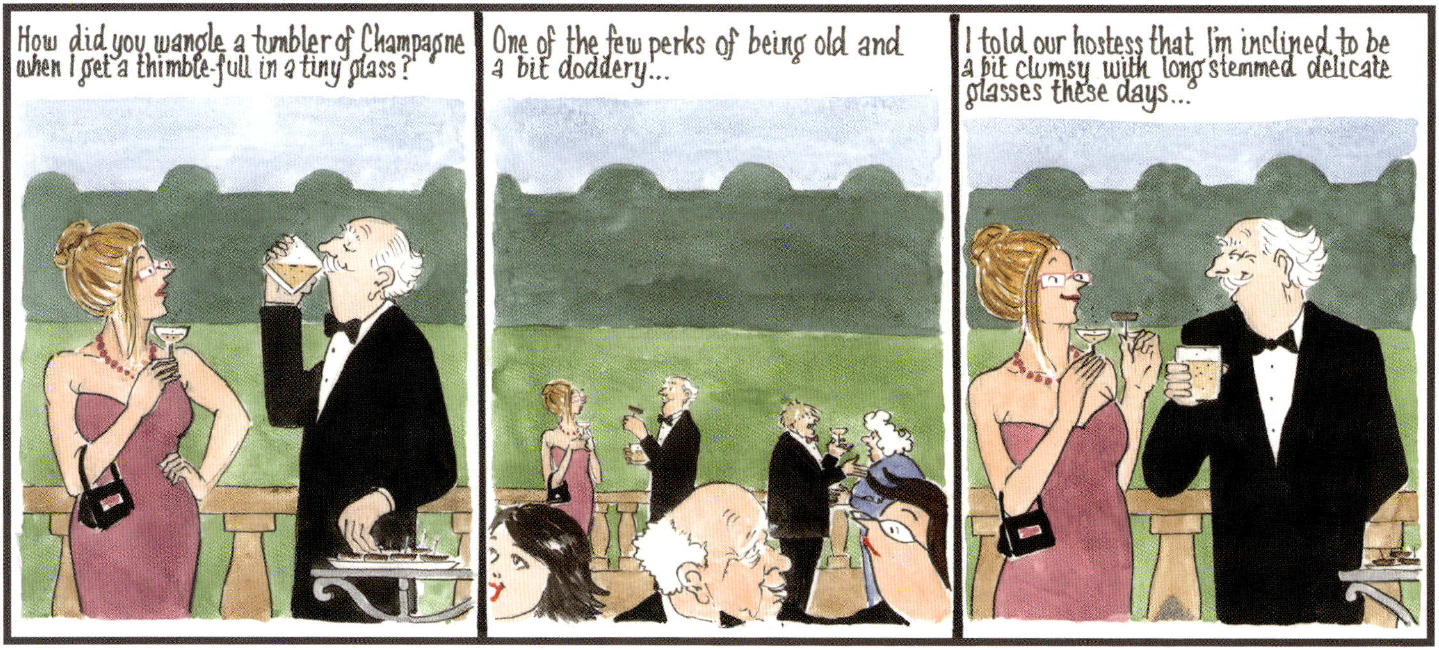
How did you wangle a tumbler of Champagne when I get a thimble-full in a tiny glass?
One of the few perks of being old and a bit doddery...
I told our hostess that I'm inclined to be a bit clumsy with long stemmed delicate glasses these days...

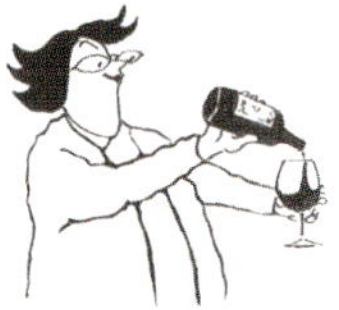

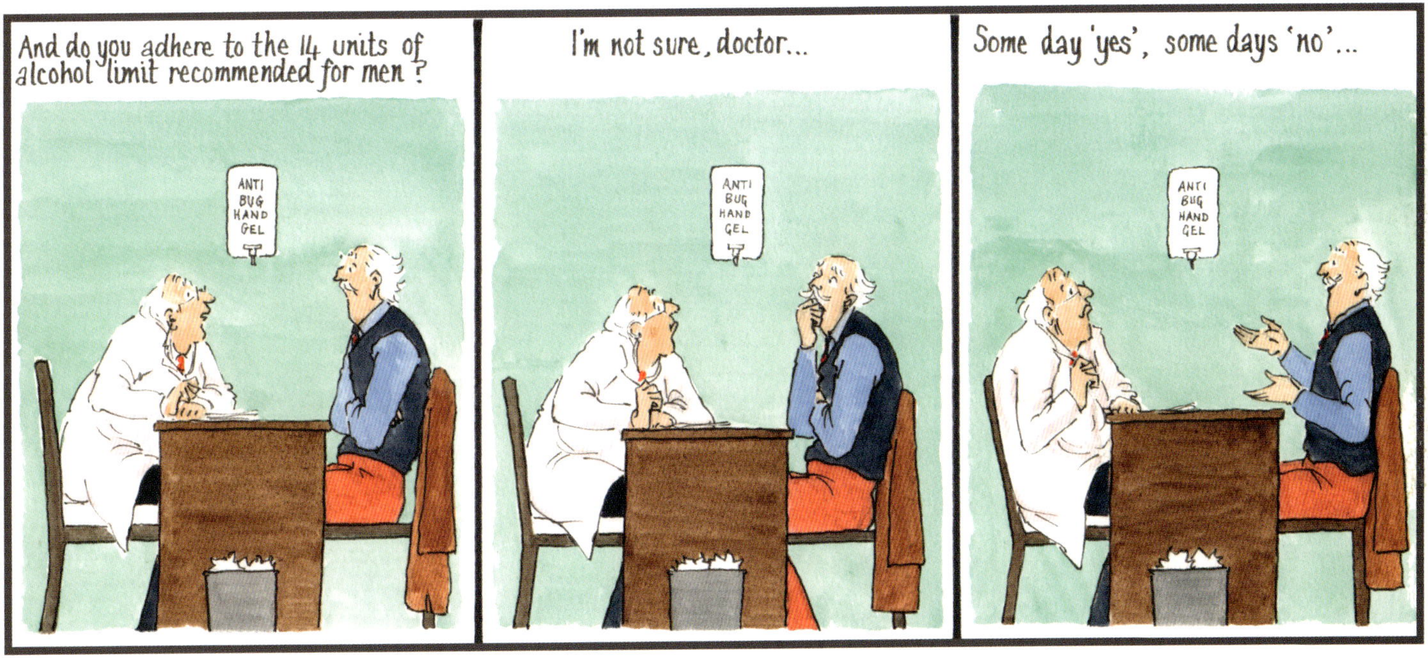
And do you adhere to the 14 units of alcohol limit recommended for men?
ANTI BUG HAND GEL
I'm not sure, doctor...
ANTI BUG HAND GEL
Some day 'yes', some days 'no'...
ANTI BUG HAND GEL

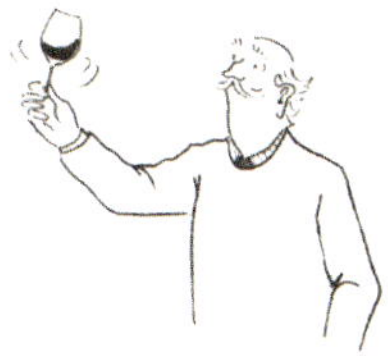

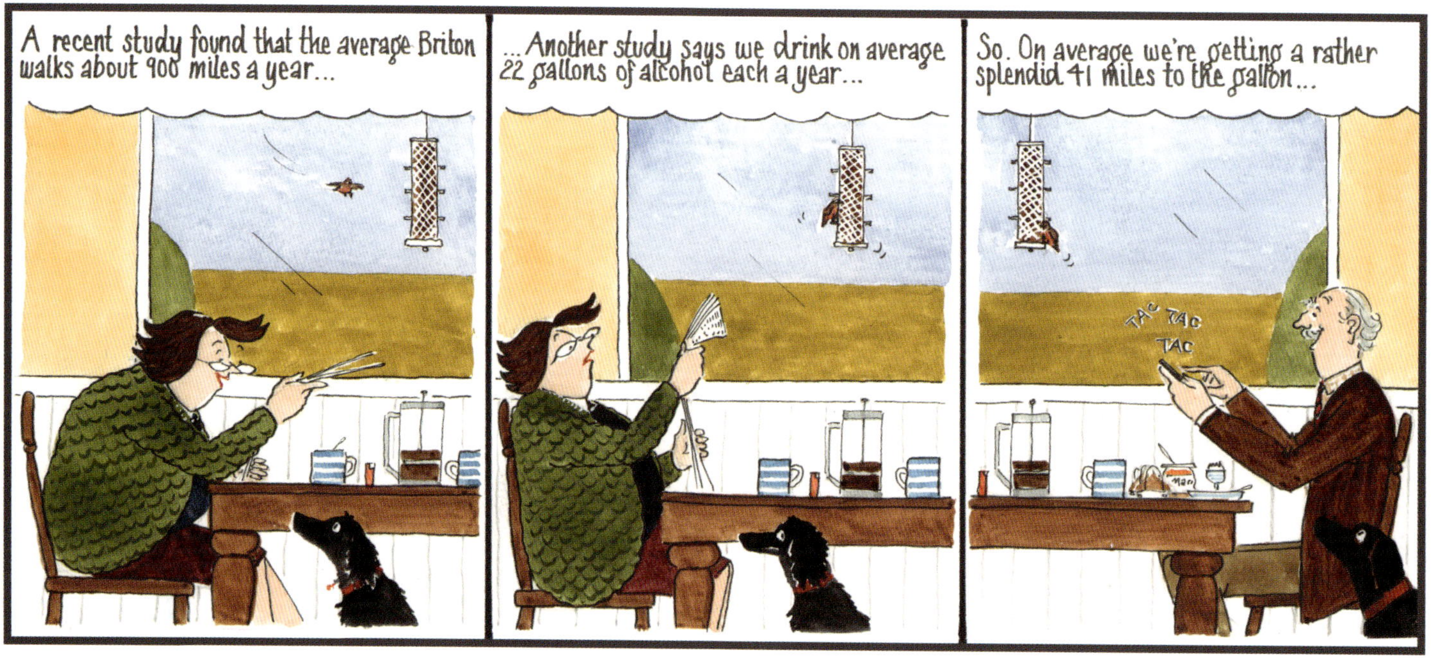
A recent study found that the average Briton walks about 900 miles a year...
...Another study says we drink on average 22 gallons of alcohol each a year...
So. On average we're getting a rather splendid 41 miles to the gallon...
TAC TAC
TAC

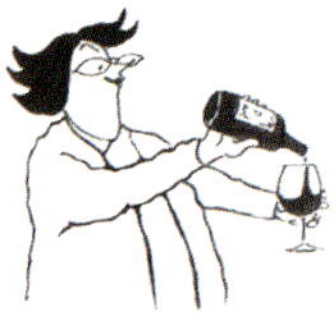

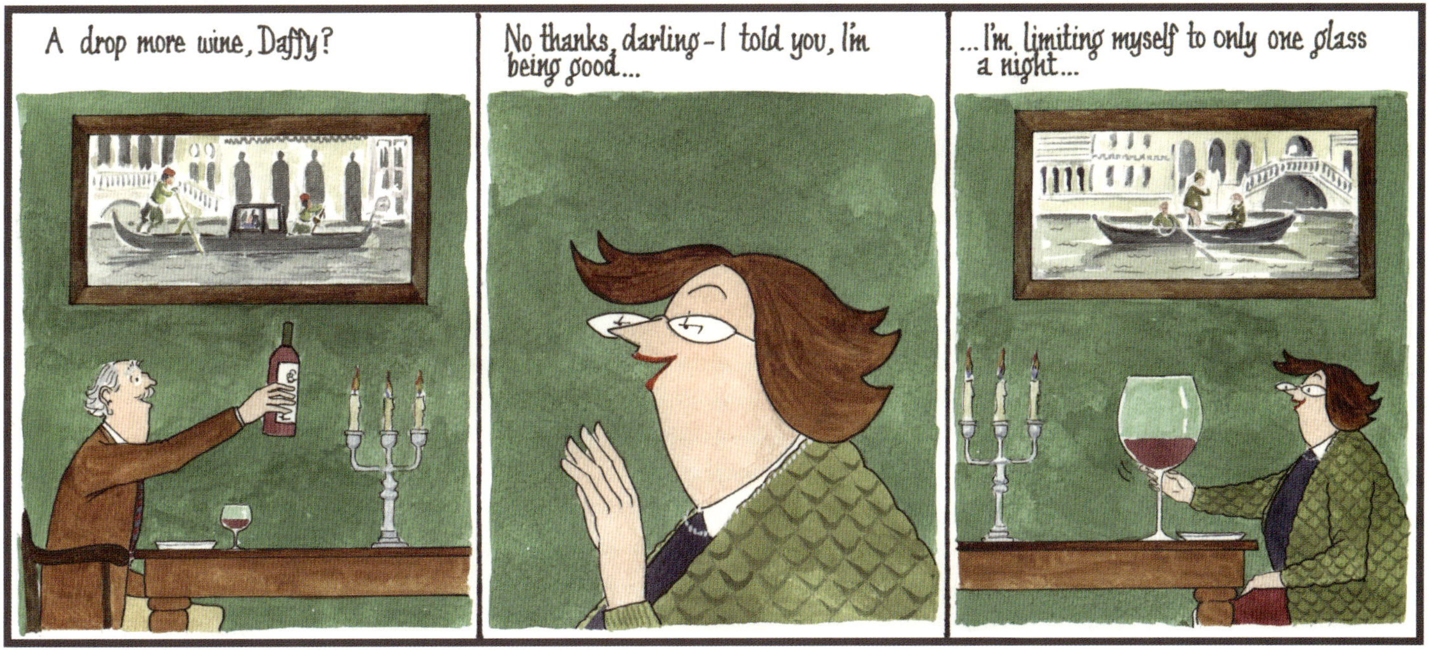
A drop more wine, Daffy?
No thanks, darling - I told you, I'm being good...
...I'm limiting myself to only one glass a night...

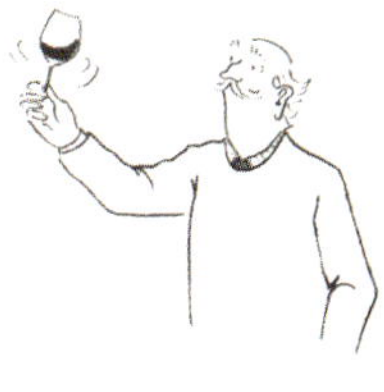

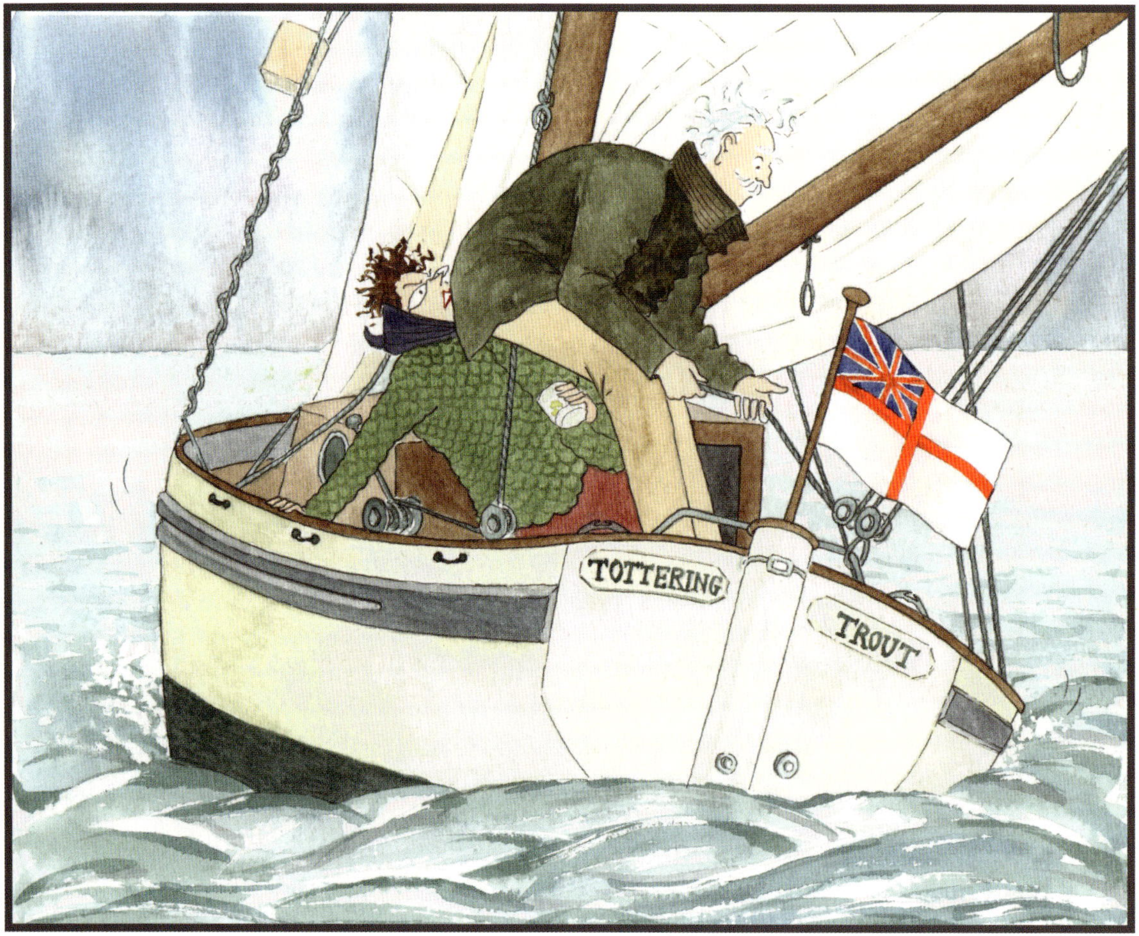
TOTTERING
TROUT

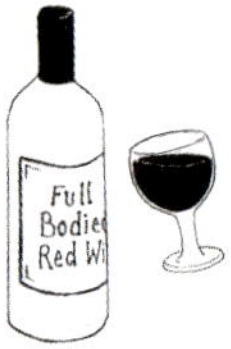
Full

" What do you mean 'get a grip?' Your bum's in my face, you've spilt my gin and my hair's gone frizzy..."

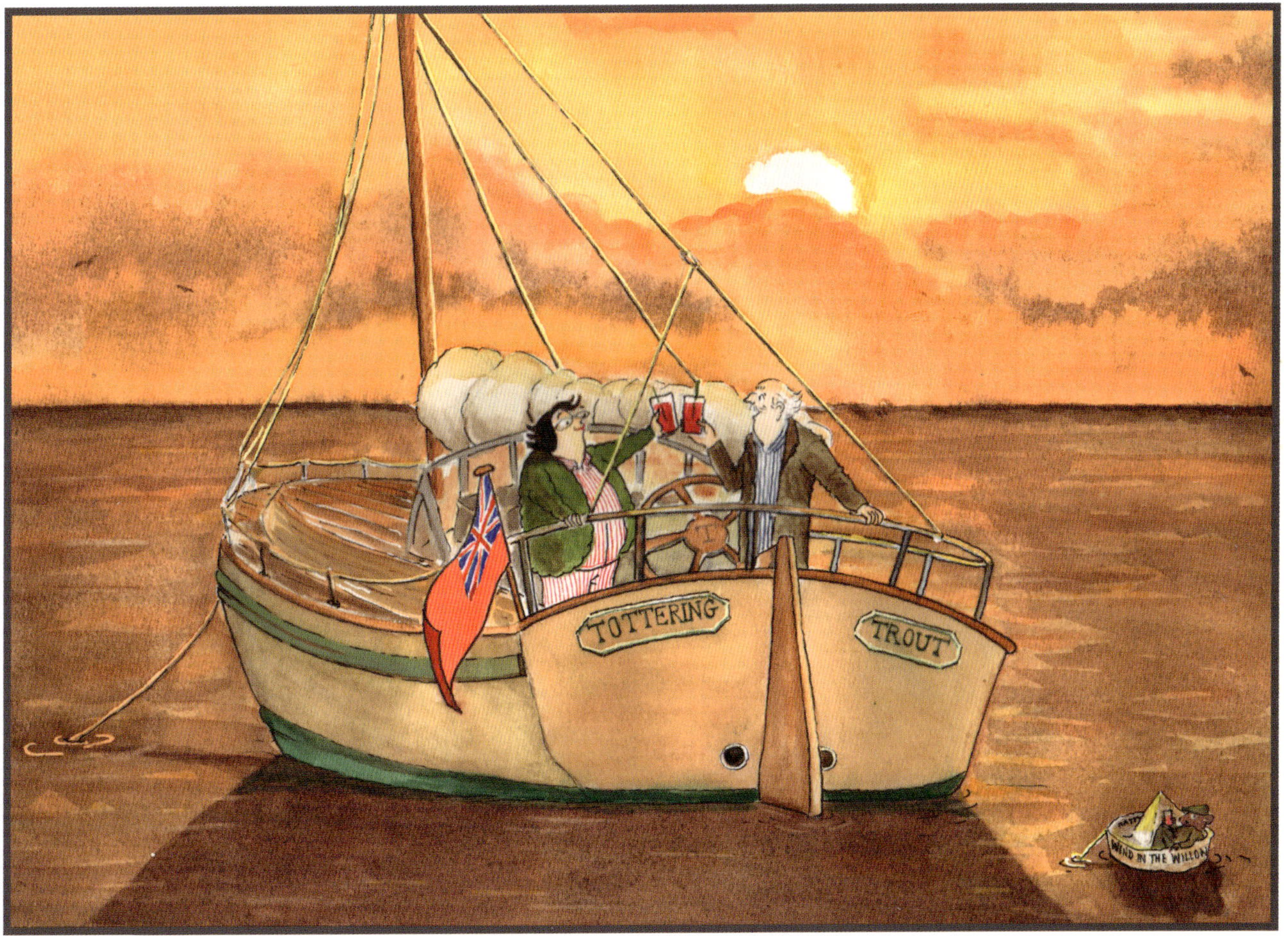
TOTTERING
TROUT

" A 'Morner' is a 'Nooner', only sooner... "

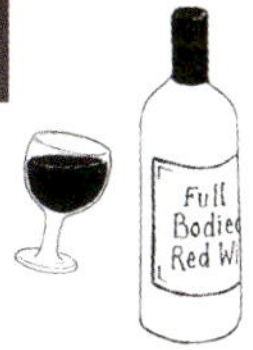
Full

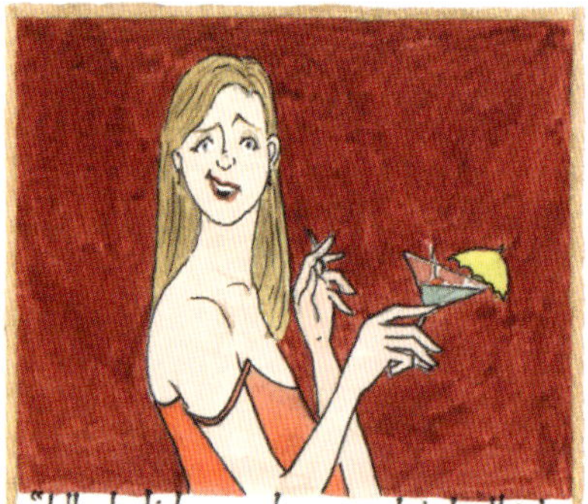

"What did you shay went into thish cocktail?.."

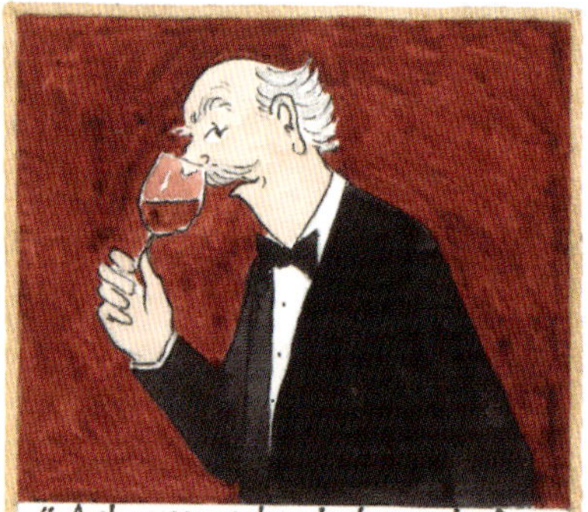

"Aah, yes - a heady bouquet of dry rot and wet Labrador..."

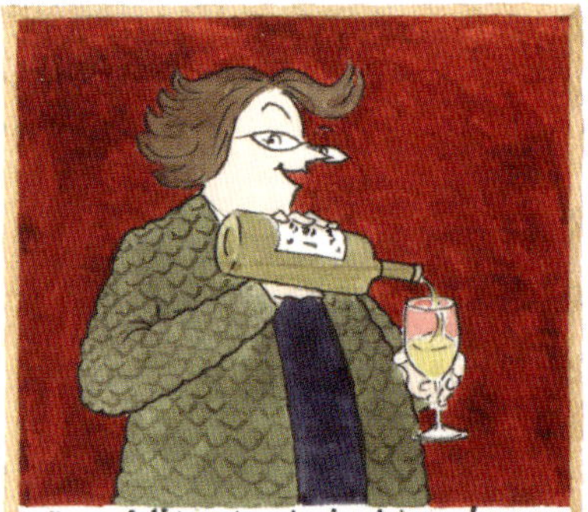

"...and this wine is best in volume with a good romantic comedy..."

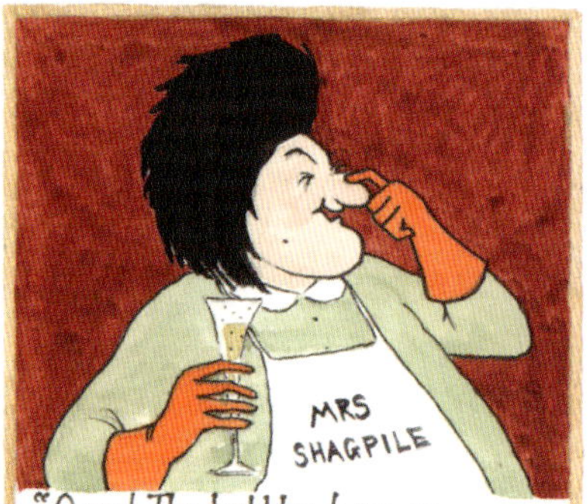
MRS SHAGPILE

"Oops! The bubbles have gone up my nose, madam..."

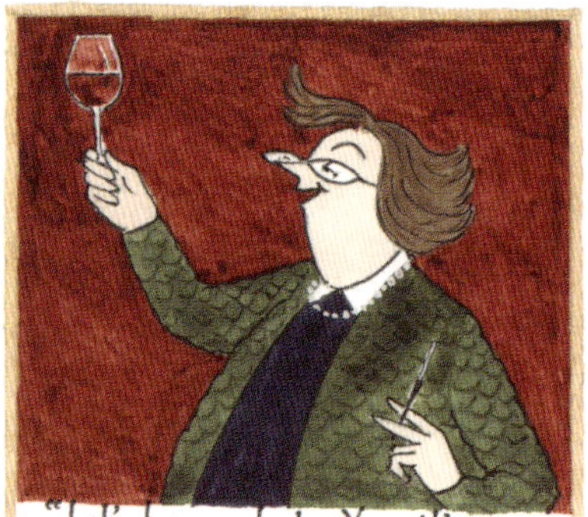

"Let's have a look - Yup - it's definitely red wine..."

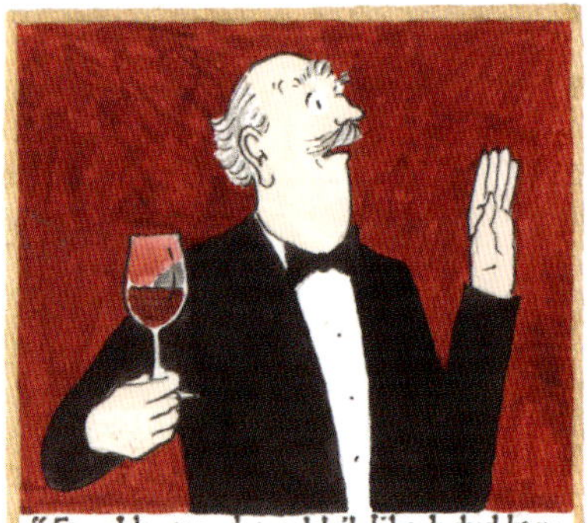

"Frankly, no - I wouldn't like baked bean flavoured crisps with my Petrus '82..."

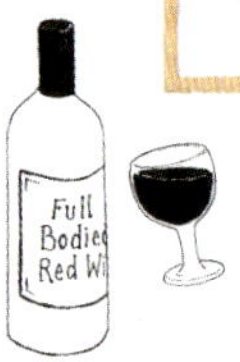
Full Bodied Red Wi

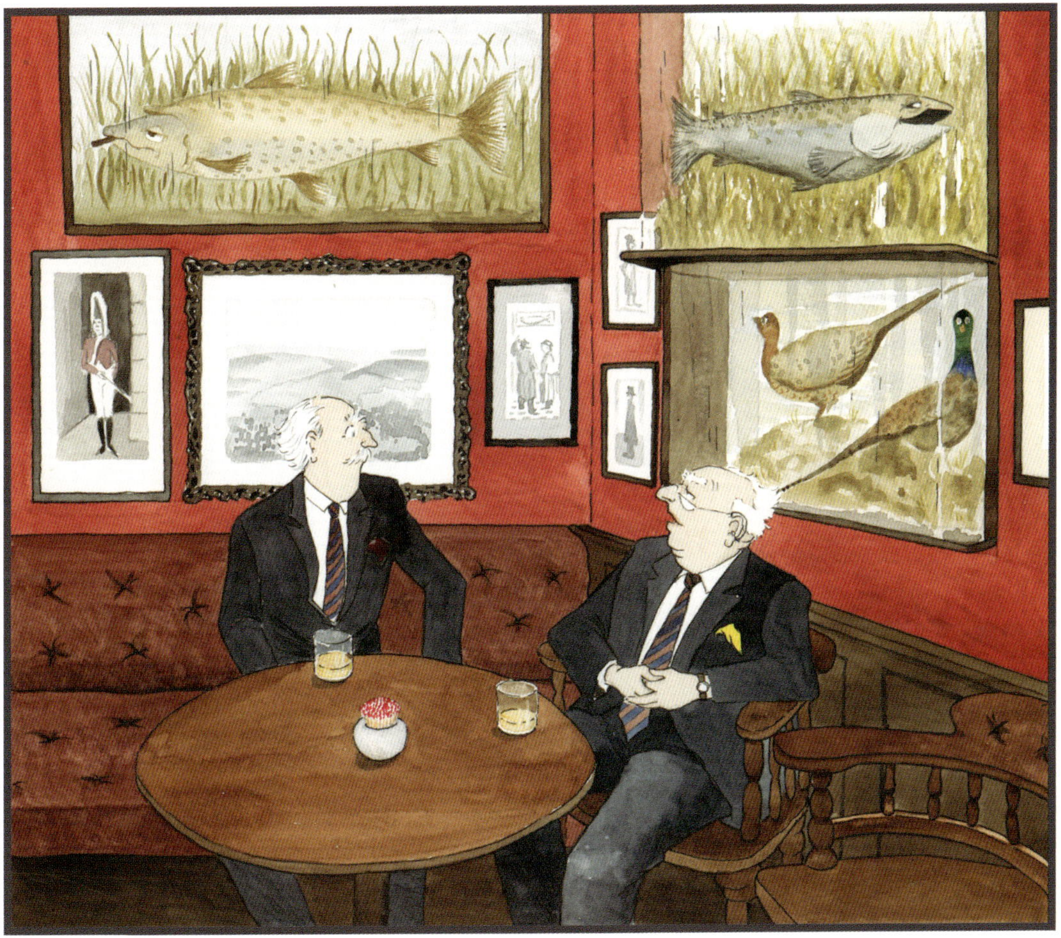

"Remind me - was it you or your brother who was killed in the war..?"

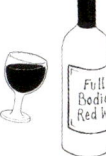

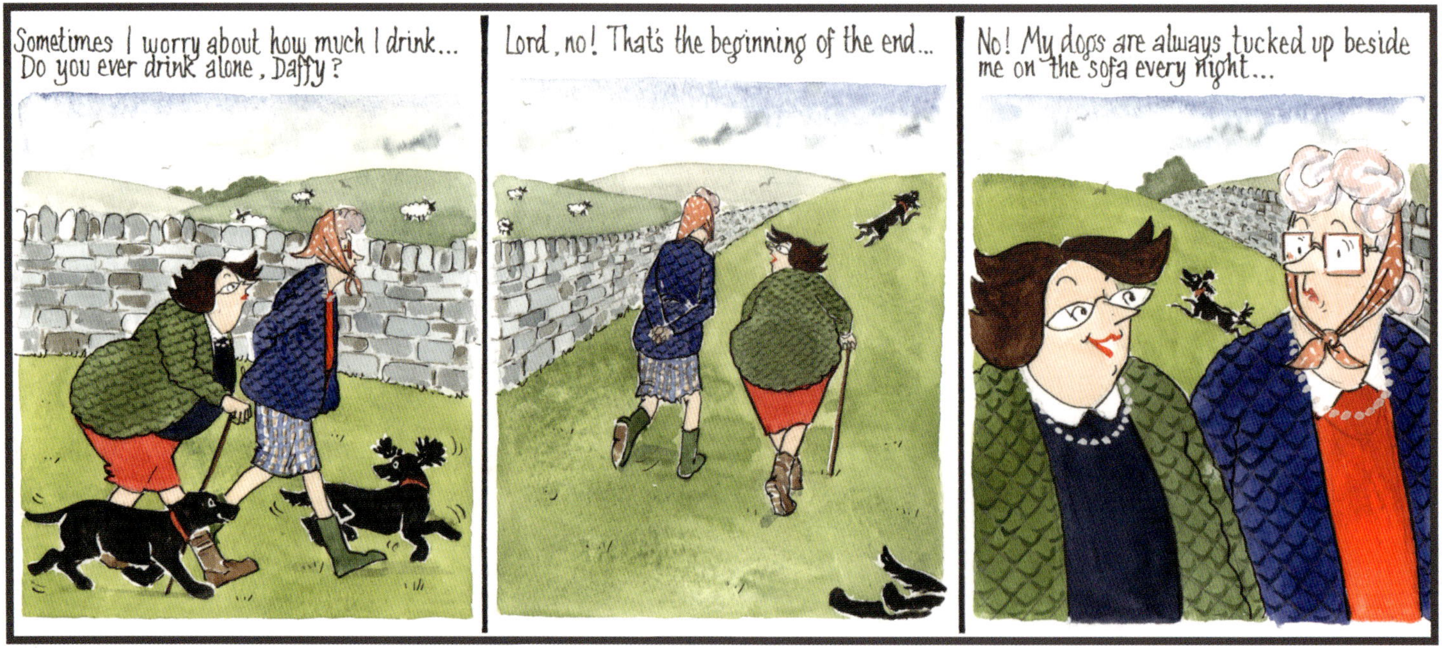
Sometimes I worry about how much I drink...
Do you ever drink alone, Daffy?
Lord, no! That's the beginning of the end...
No! My dogs are always tucked up beside me on the sofa every night...

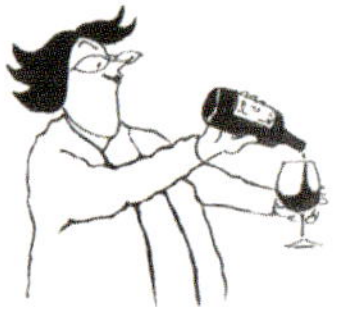

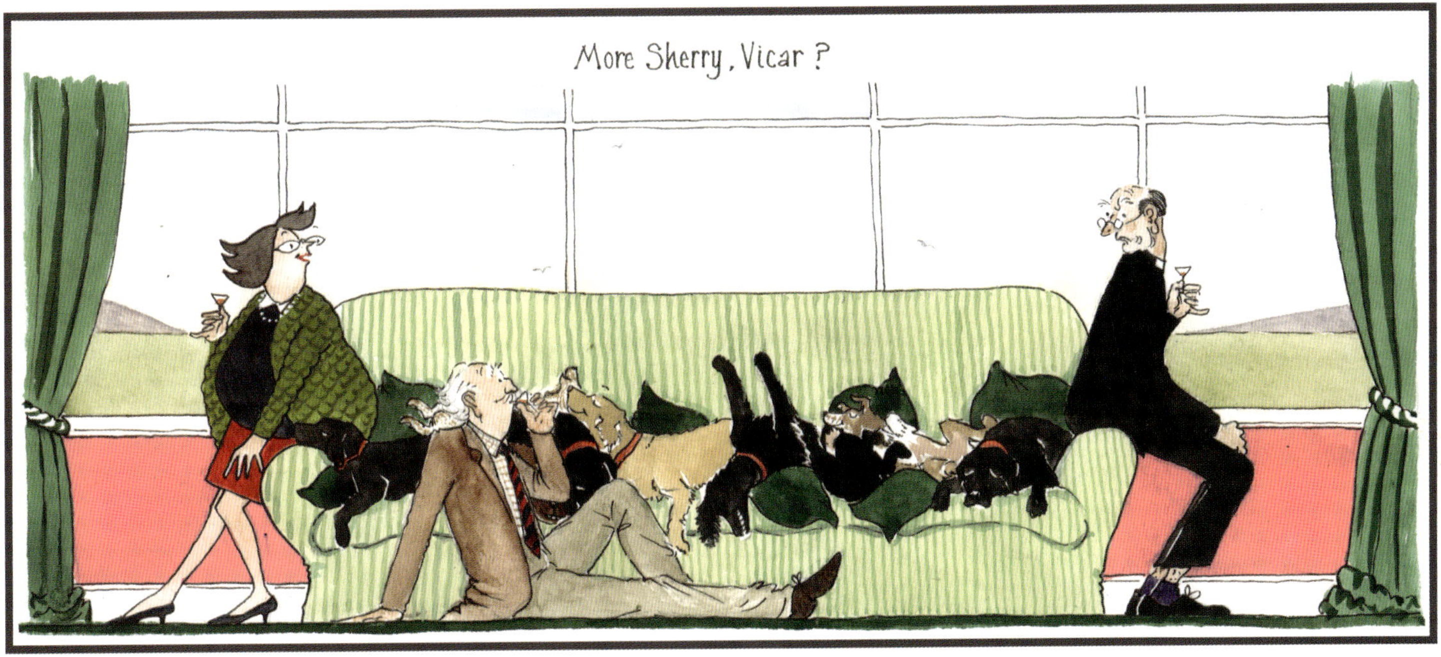

More Sherry, Vicar?

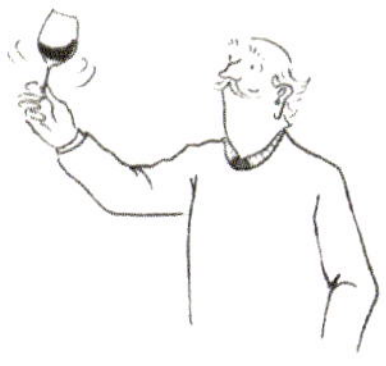

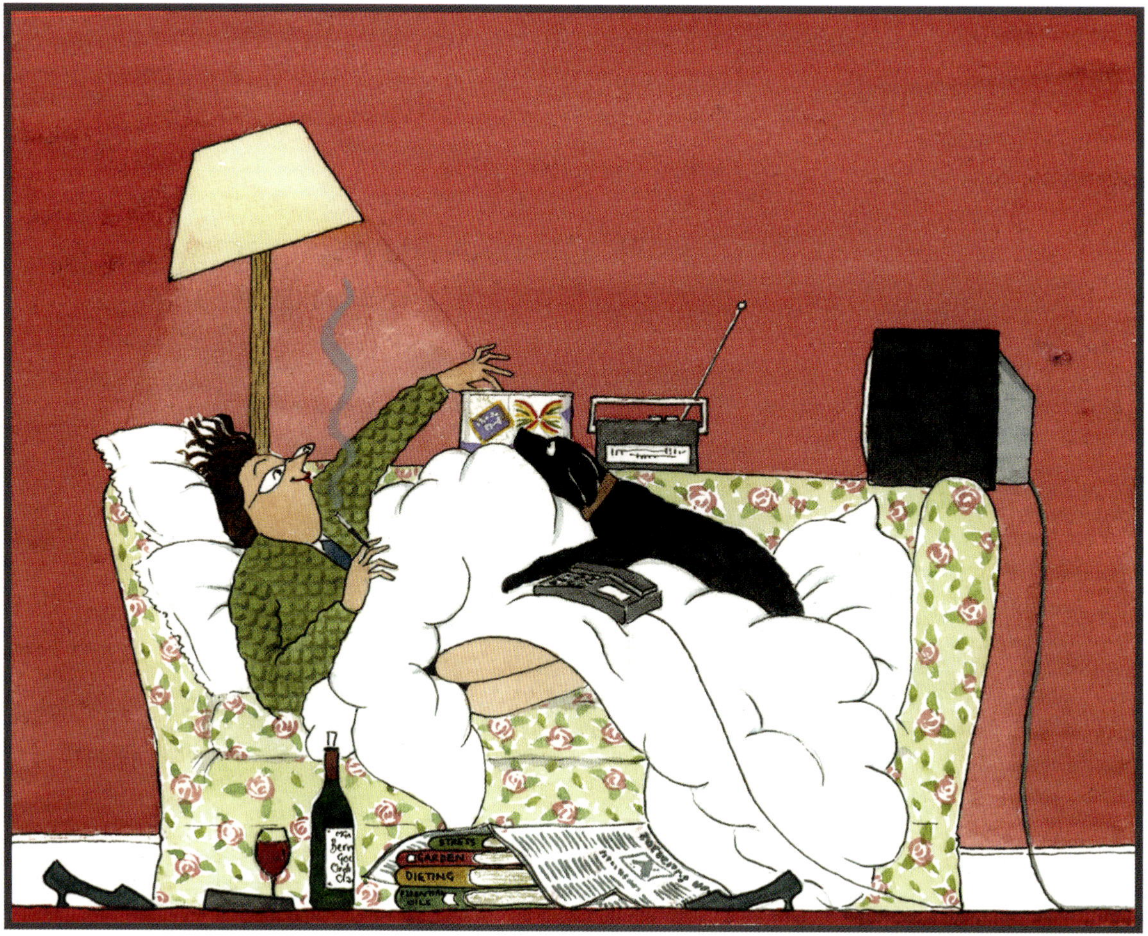
STRESS
GARDEN
DIETING

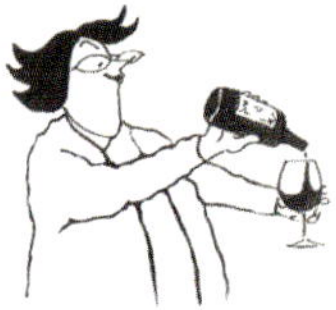

THE FEMALE CHARACTER: A deep sense of gratitude for the institution of the Gentleman's Club...

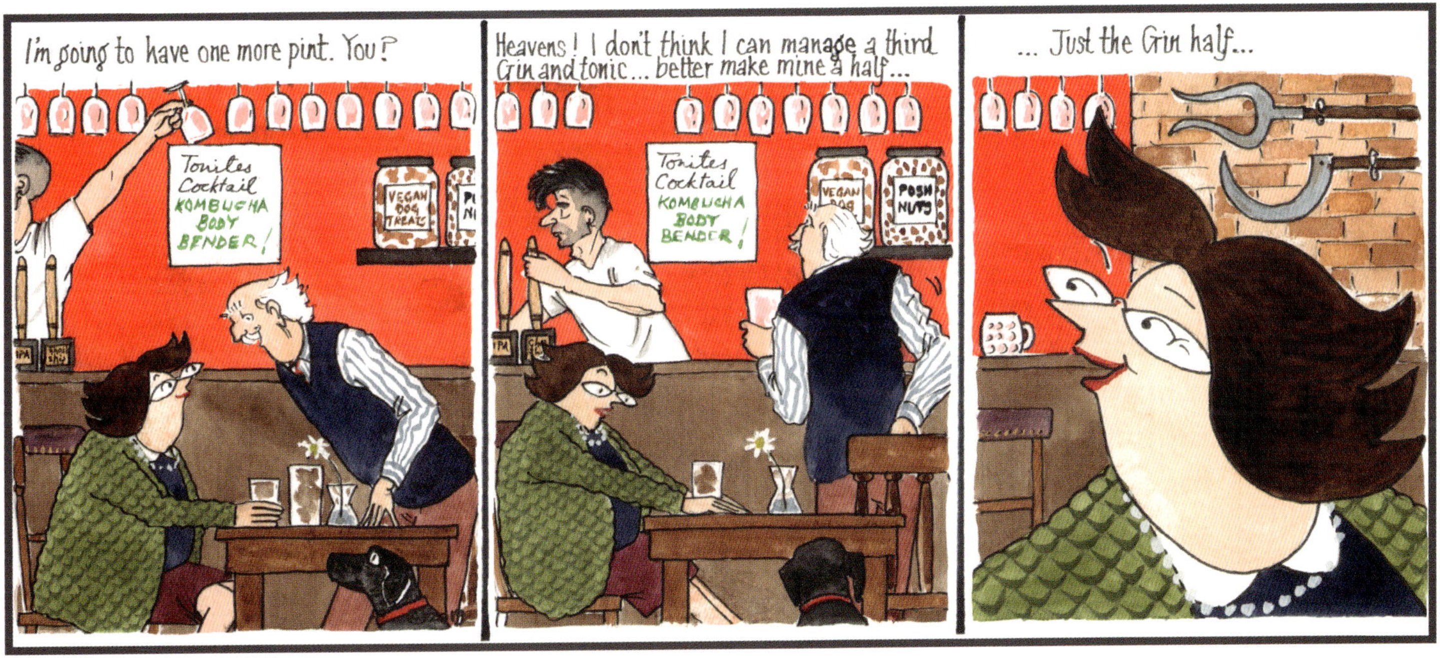
I'm going to have one more pint. You?
Tonites Cocktail
KOMBUCHA BODY BENDER!
VEGAN DOG TREATS
Heavens! I don't think I can manage a third Gin and tonic... better make mine a half...
Tonites Cocktail
KOMBUCHA BODY BENDER!
POSH NUTS
... Just the Gin half...

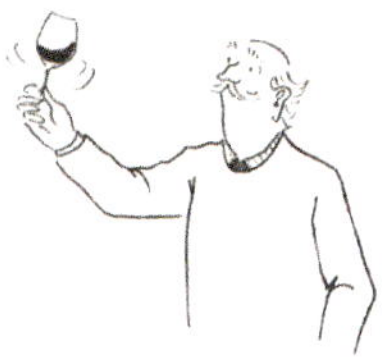

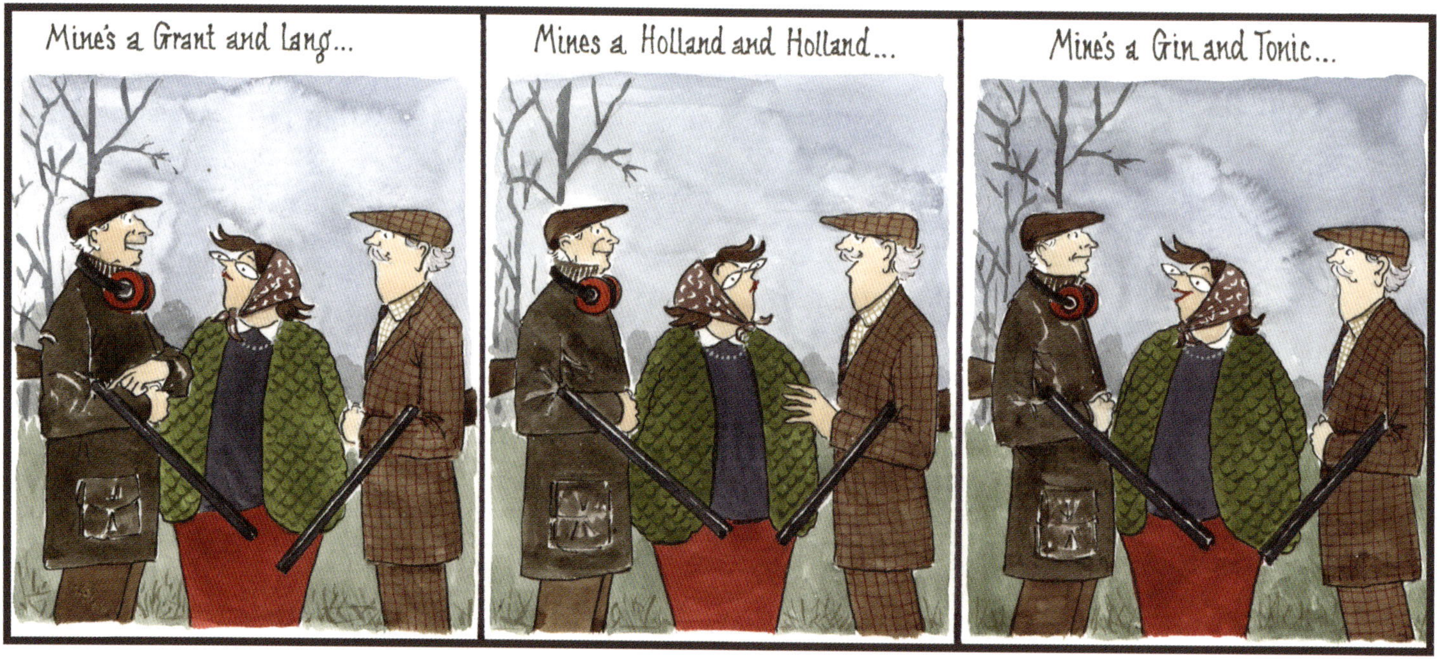
Mine's a Grant and lang...
Mines a Holland and Holland...
Mine's a Gin and Tonic...

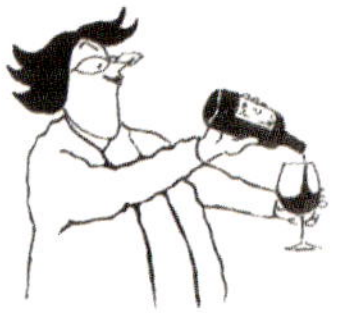

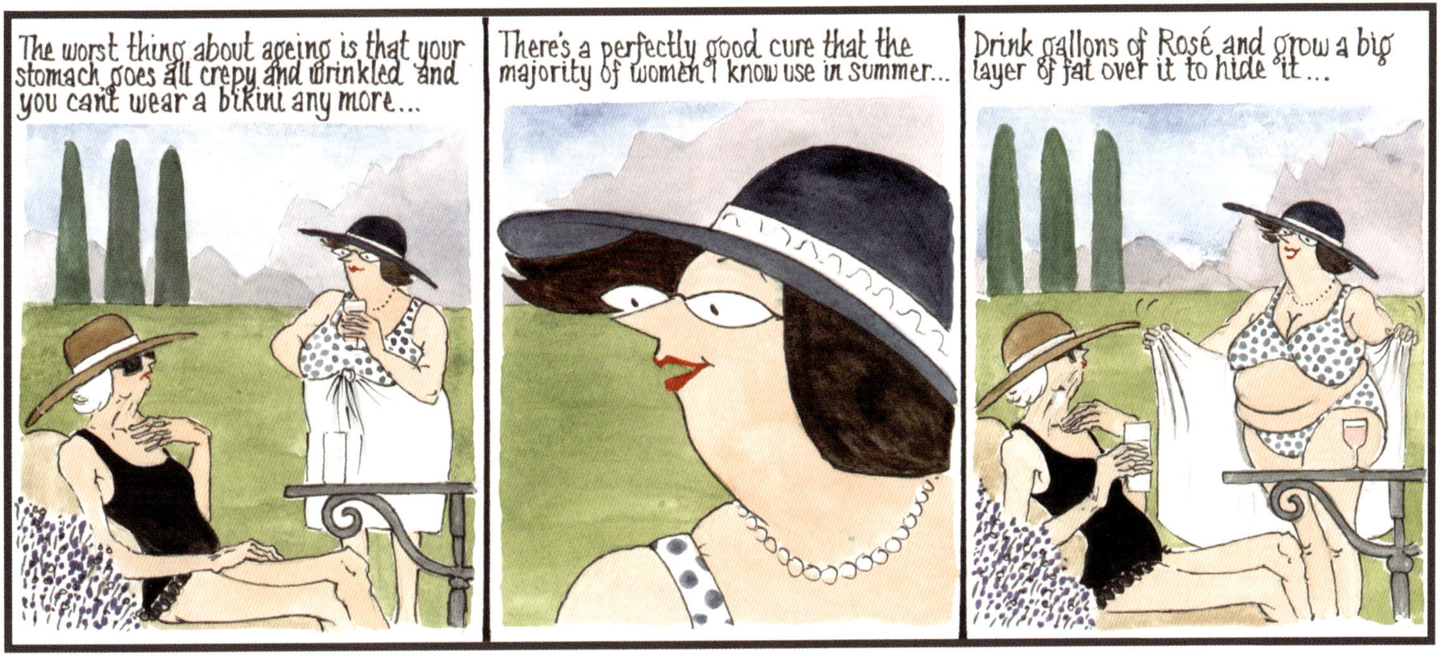
The worst thing about ageing is that your stomach goes all crepy and wrinkled and you can't wear a bikini any more...
There's a perfectly good cure that the majority of women I know use in summer...
Drink gallons of Rosé and grow a big layer of fat over it to hide it...

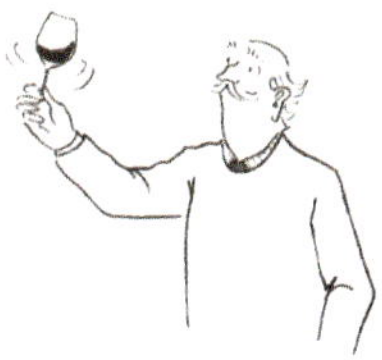

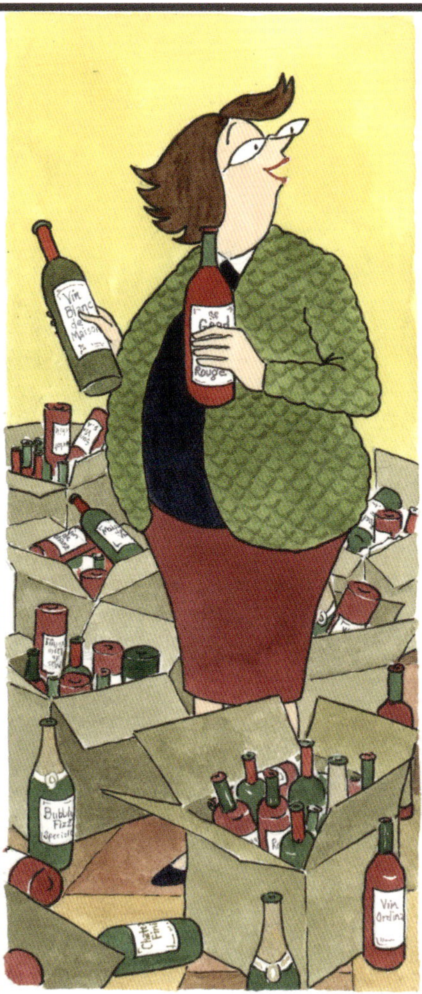
Vin Blanc
Good
Rouge
Bubbly Fizz

"I think it's time we went to the bottle bank, darlings..."

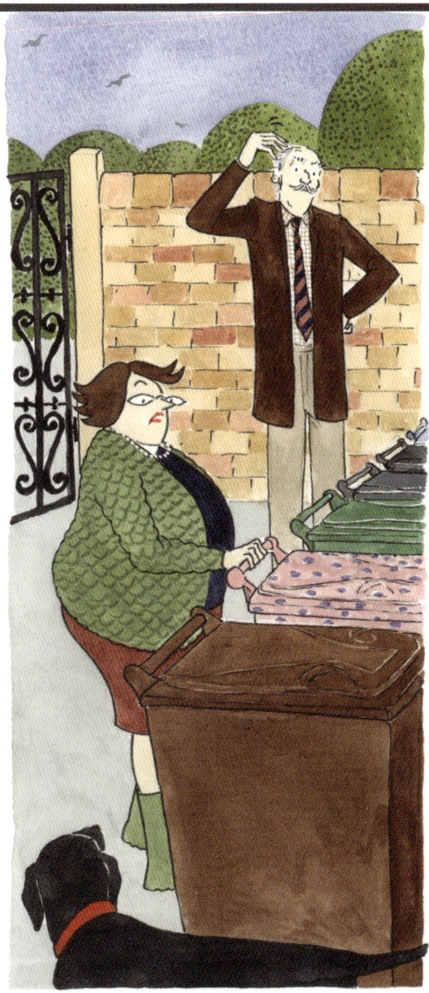

"3rd Tuesday of the 5th month- is that this pink bin with purple spots for Champagne corks and take away curry containers only?.."

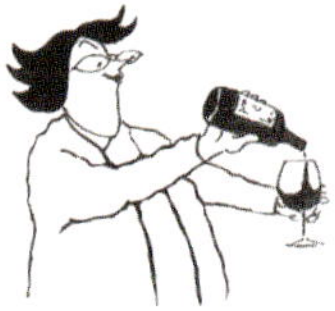

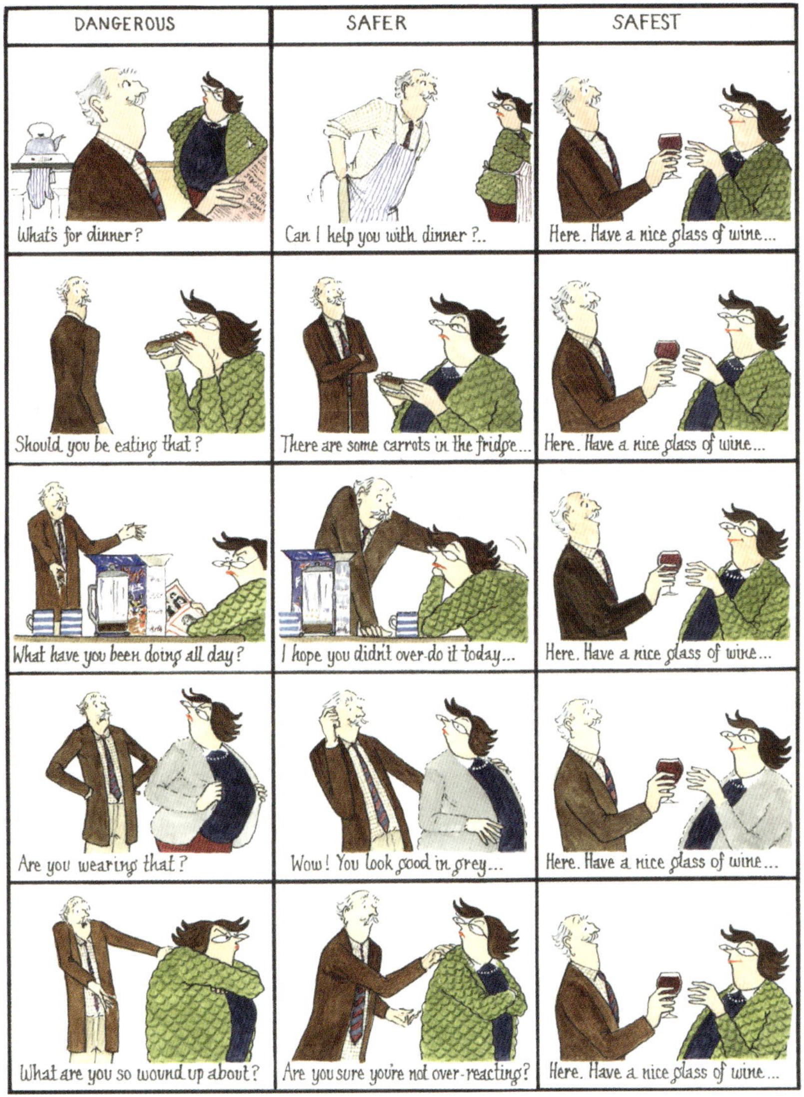
DANGEROUS
SAFER
SAFEST
What's for dinner?
Can I help you with dinner?..
Here. Have a nice glass of wine...
Should you be eating that?
There are some carrots in the fridge...
Here. Have a nice glass of wine...
What have you been doing all day?
I hope you didn't over-do it today...
Here. Have a nice glass of wine...
Are you wearing that?
Wow! You look good in grey...
Here. Have a nice glass of wine...
What are you so wound up about?
Are you sure you're not over-reacting?
Here. Have a nice glass of wine...

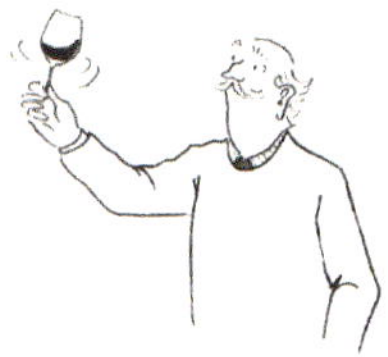

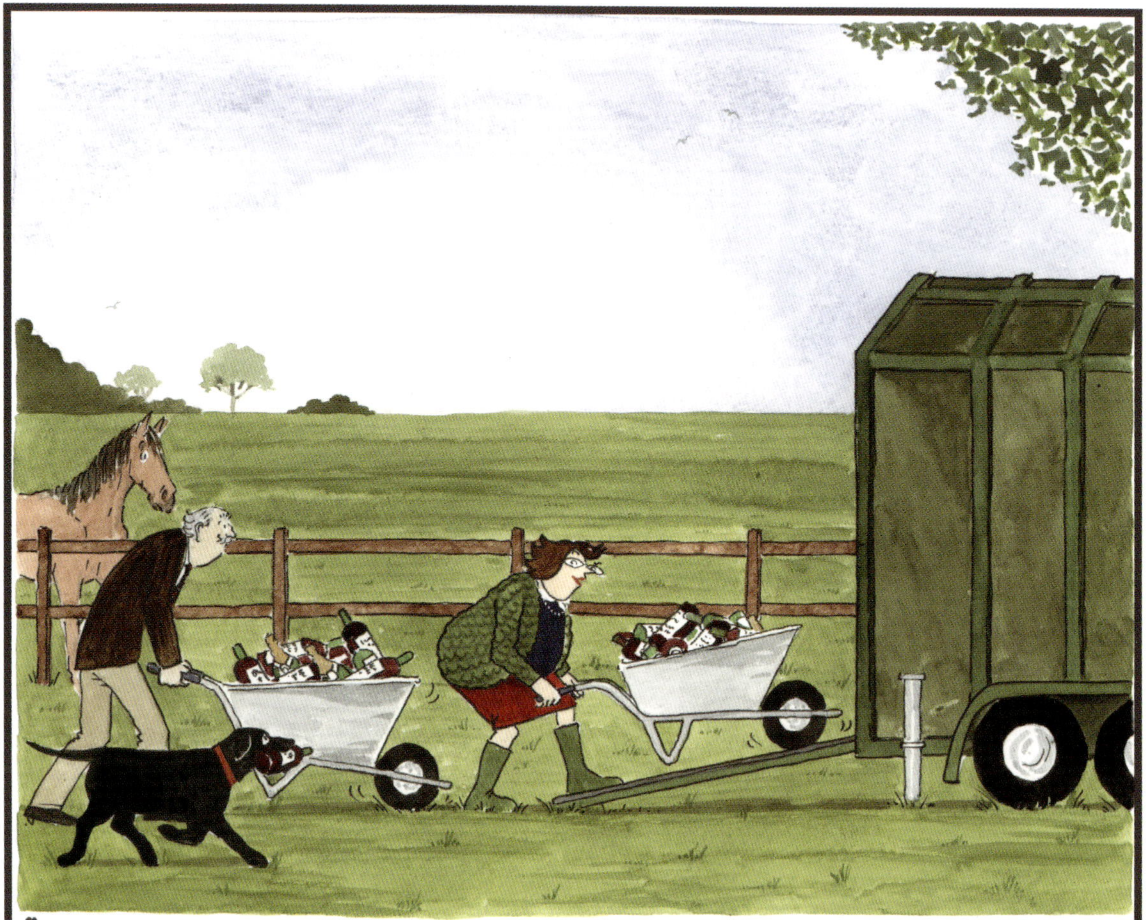

"How on earth do people without horse boxes cope with a trip to the bottle bank after a good dinner party?"

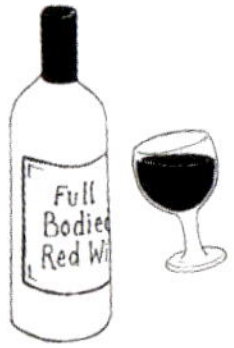
Full

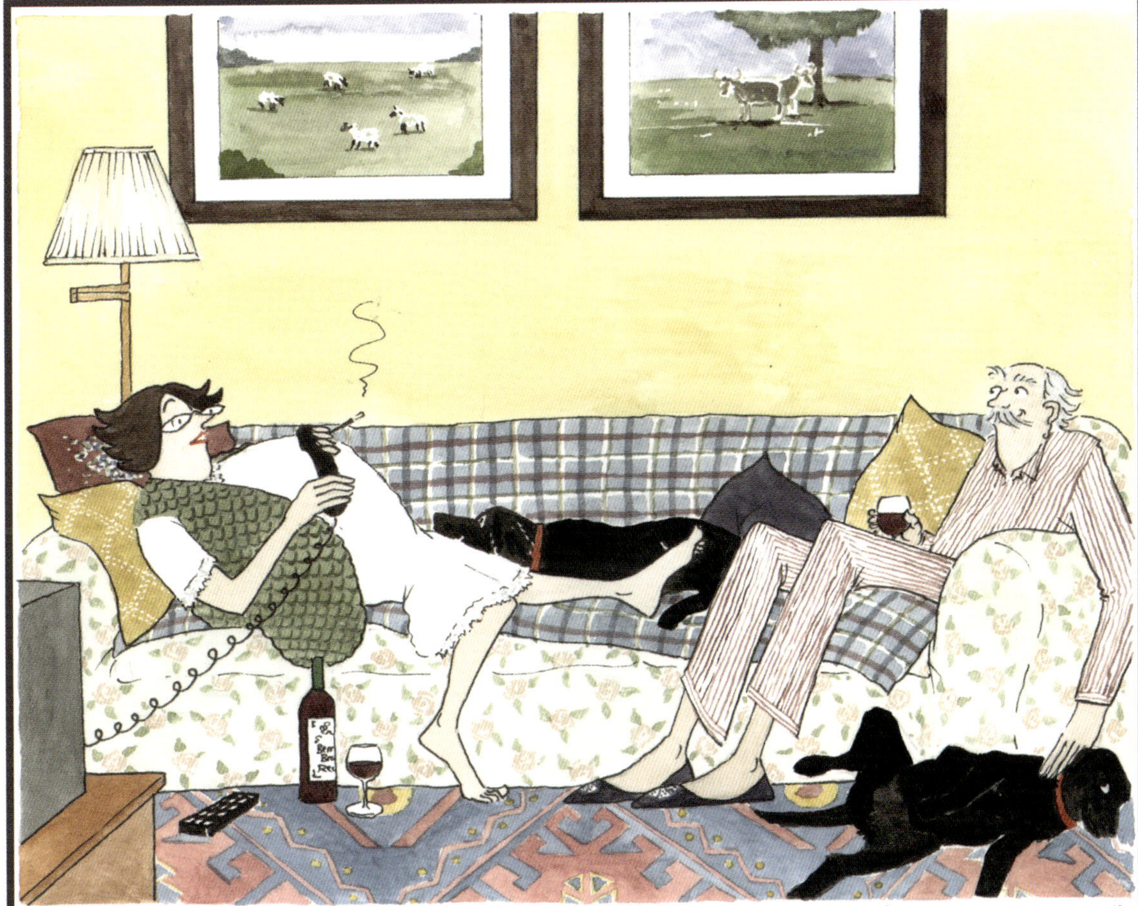

"Are we running late or have we forgotten we were due for dinner at 8 with the Eameaux-Chavs?.."

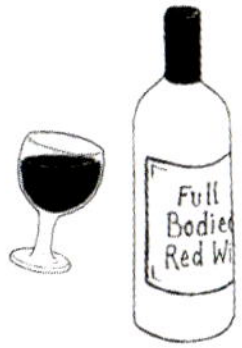
Full

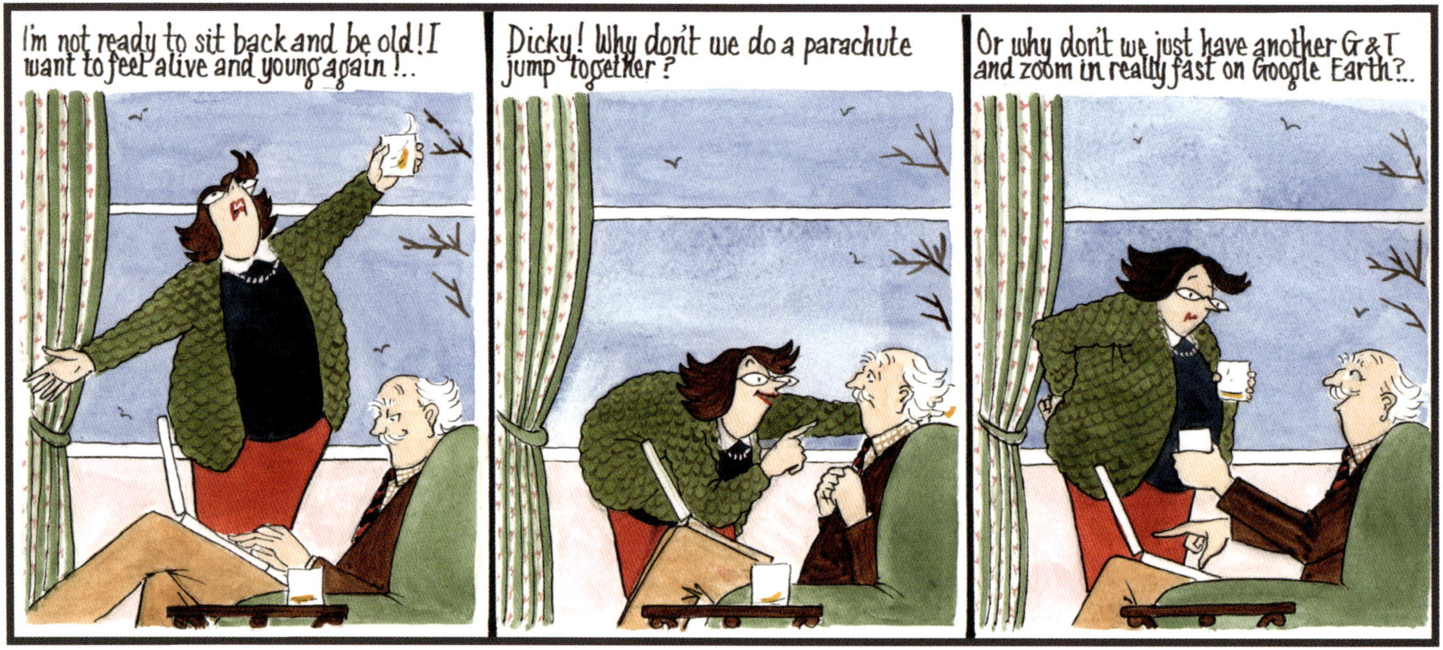
I'm not ready to sit back and be old! I want to feel alive and young again!..
Dicky! Why don't we do a parachute jump together?
Or why don't we just have another G&T and zoom in really fast on Google Earth?..

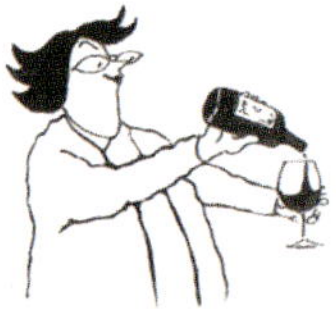

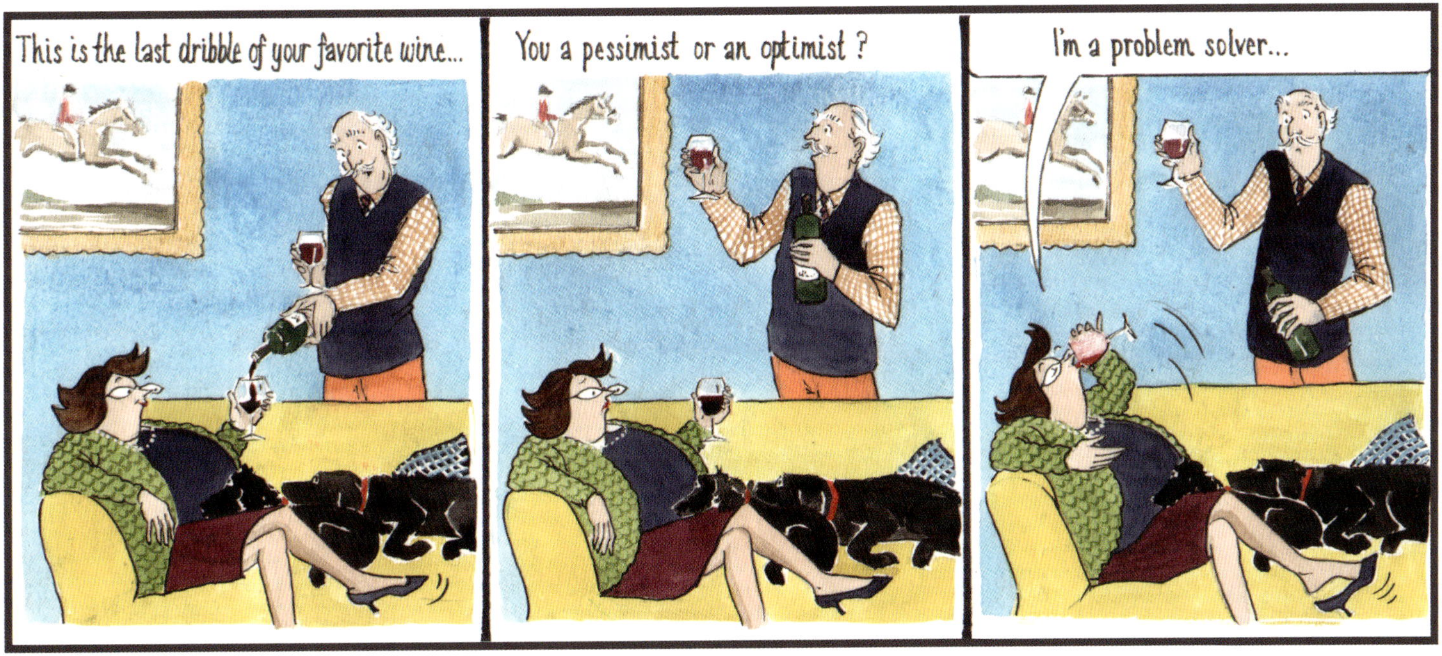
This is the last dribble of your favorite wine...
You a pessimist or an optimist ?
I'm a problem solver...

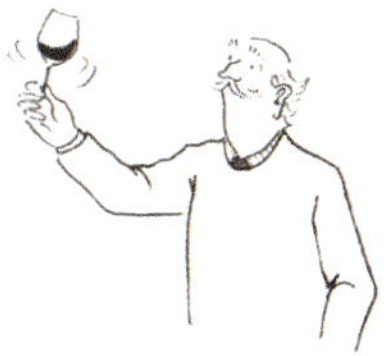

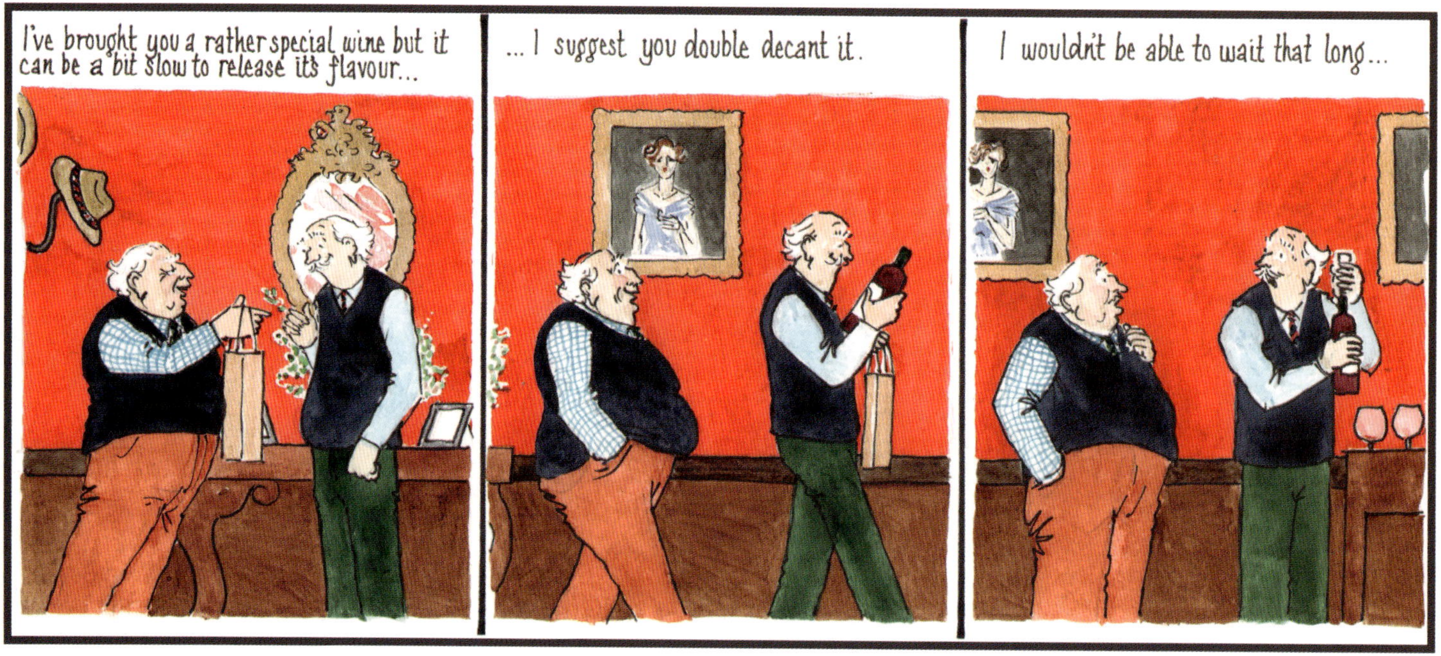

I've brought you a rather special wine but it can be a bit slow to release its flavour...
... I suggest you double decant it.
I wouldn't be able to wait that long...

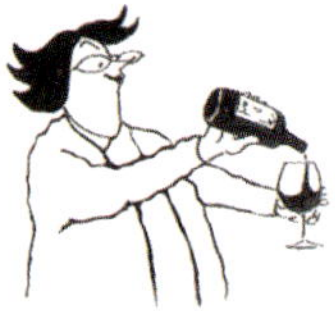

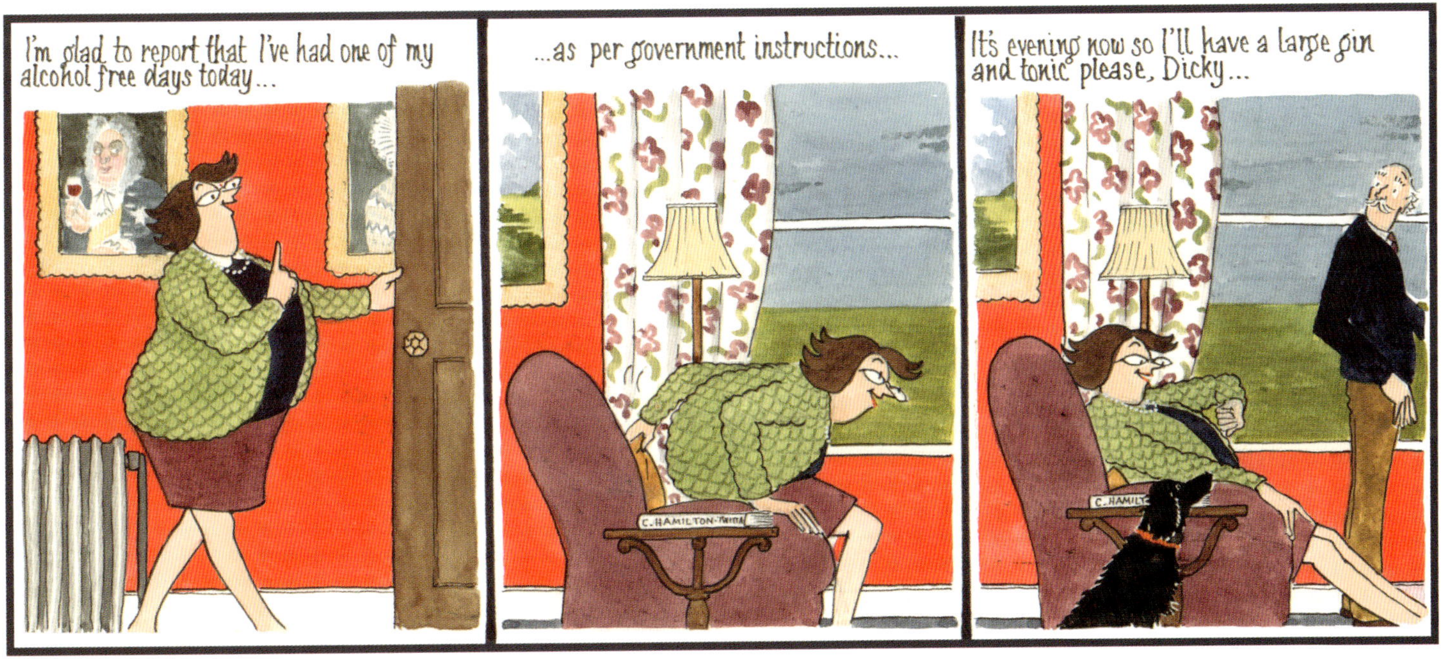
I'm glad to report that I've had one of my alcohol free days today...
...as per government instructions...
It's evening now so I'll have a large gin and tonic please, Dicky...
C. HAMILTON-

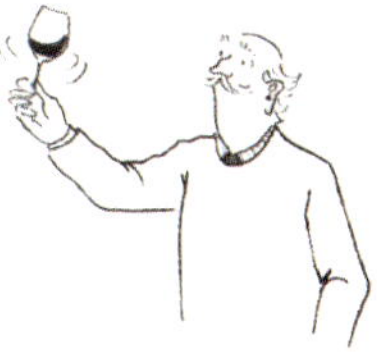

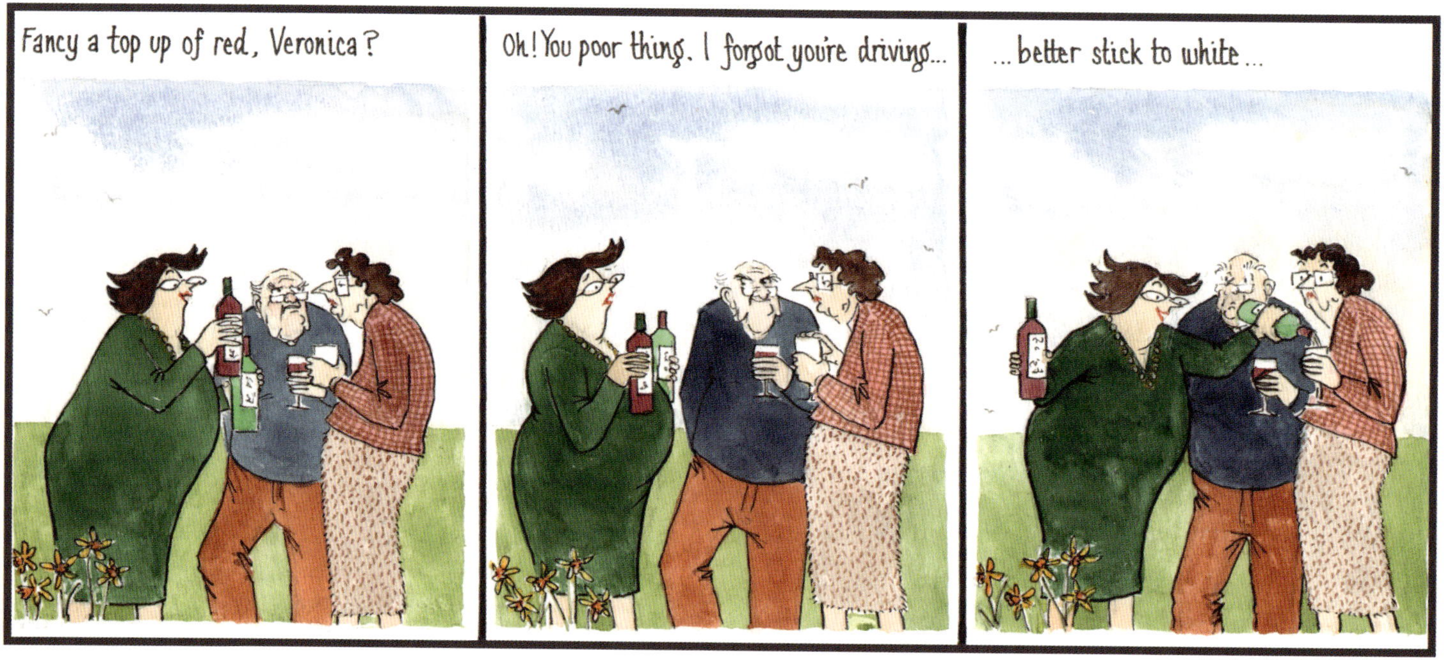
Fancy a top up of red, Veronica?
Oh! You poor thing. I forgot you're driving...
... better stick to white ...

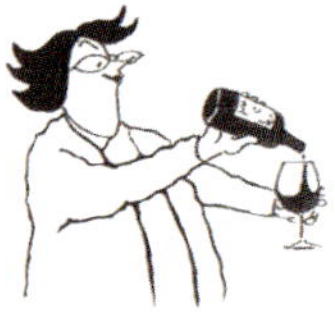

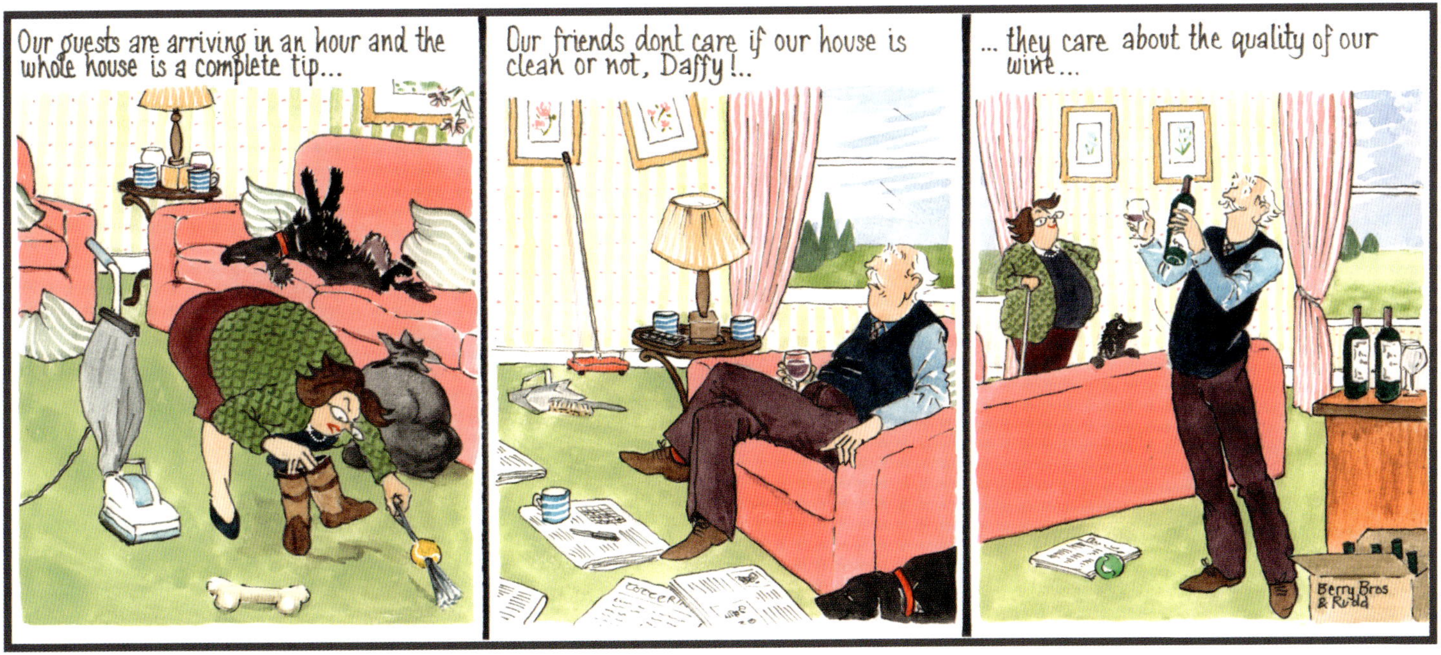
Our guests are arriving in an hour and the whole house is a complete tip...
Our friends dont care if our house is clean or not, Daffy!..
... they care about the quality of our wine...
Berry Bros & Rudd

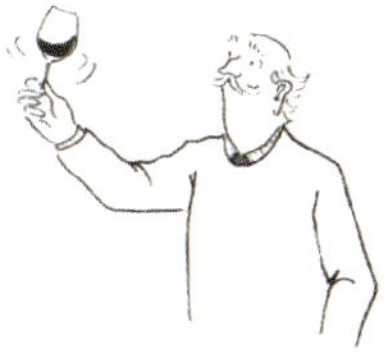

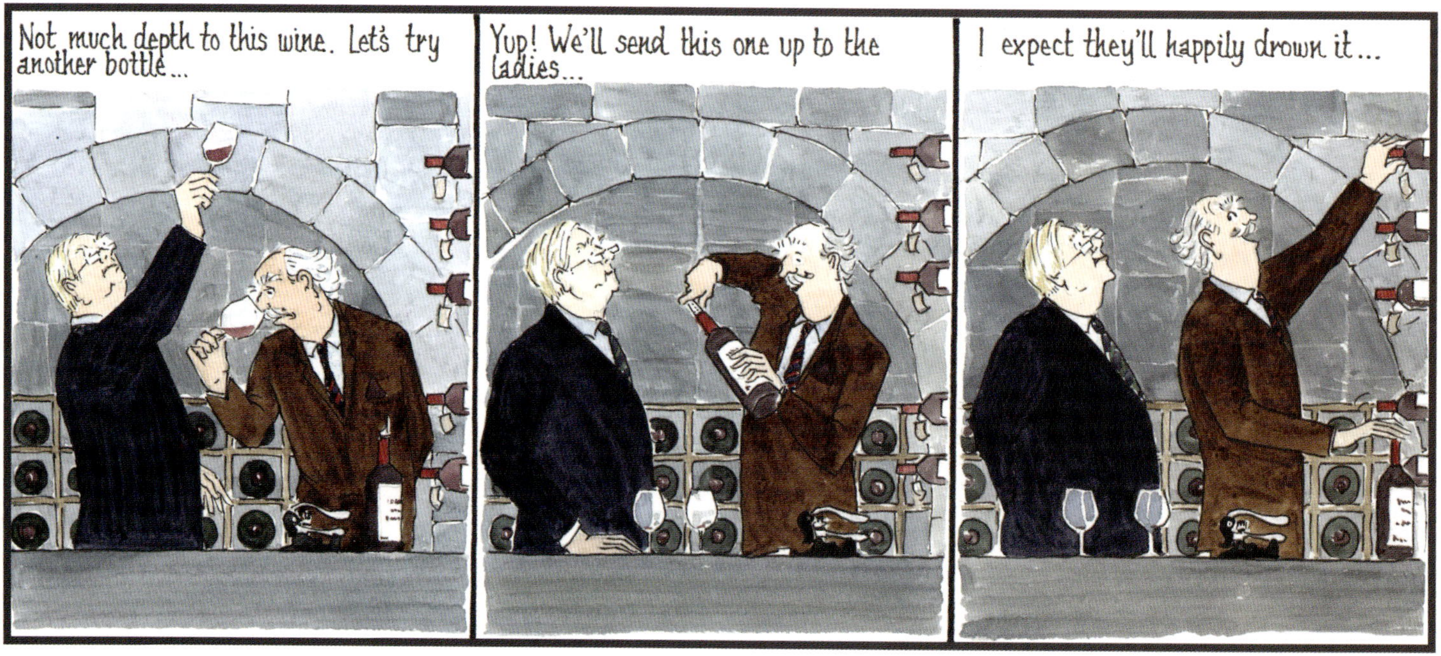
Not much depth to this wine. Let's try another bottle...
Yup! We'll send this one up to the ladies...
I expect they'll happily drown it...

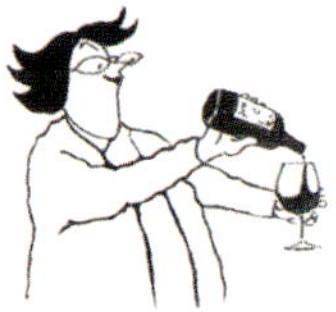

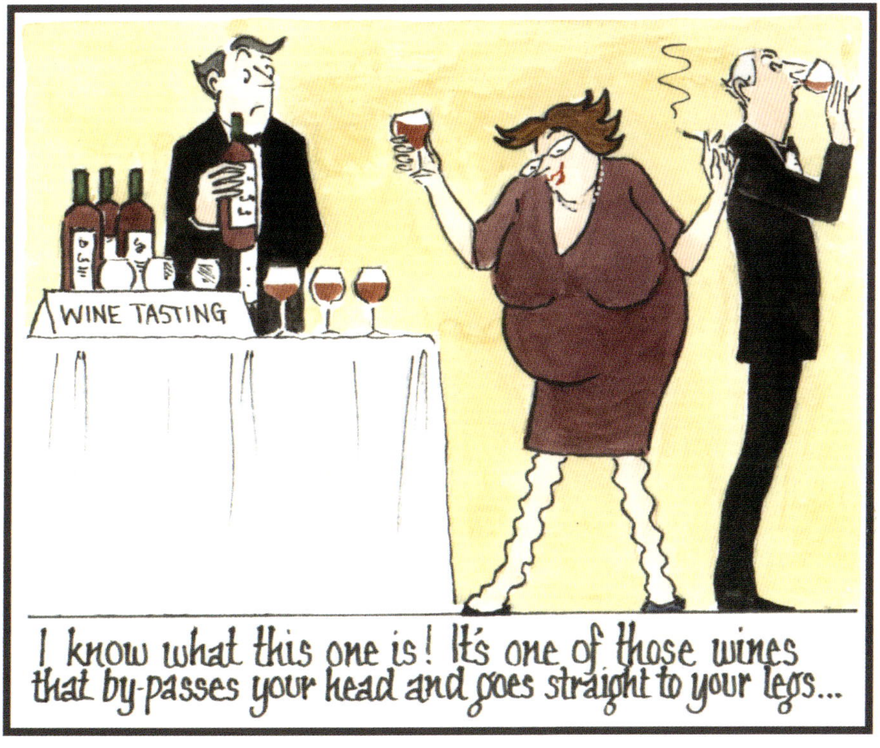

WINE TASTING

I know what this one is! It's one of those wines that by-passes your head and goes straight to your legs...

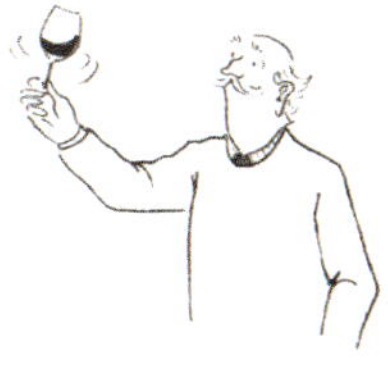

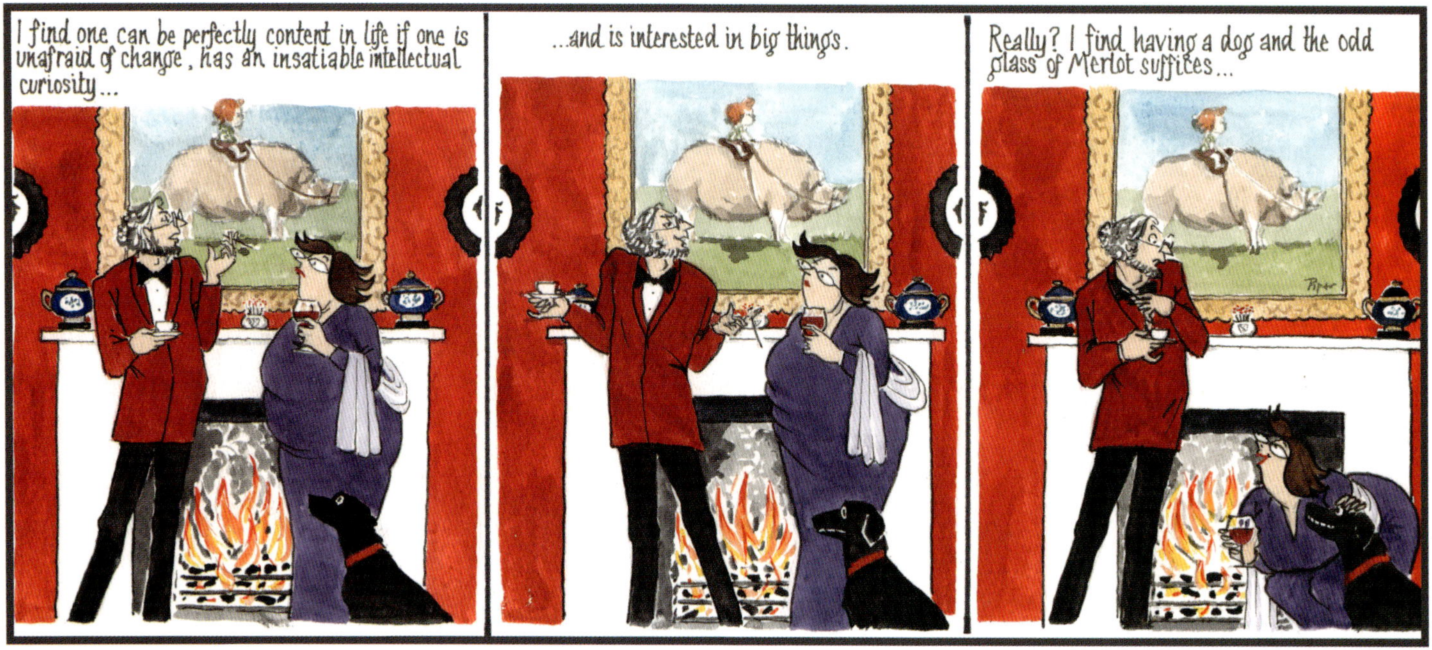
I find one can be perfectly content in life if one is unafraid of change, has an insatiable intellectual curiosity...
...and is interested in big things.
Really? I find having a dog and the odd glass of Merlot suffices...

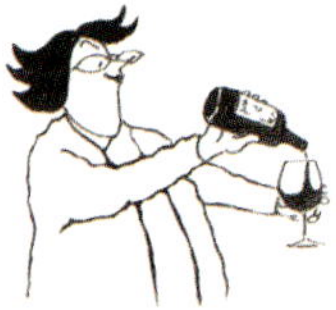

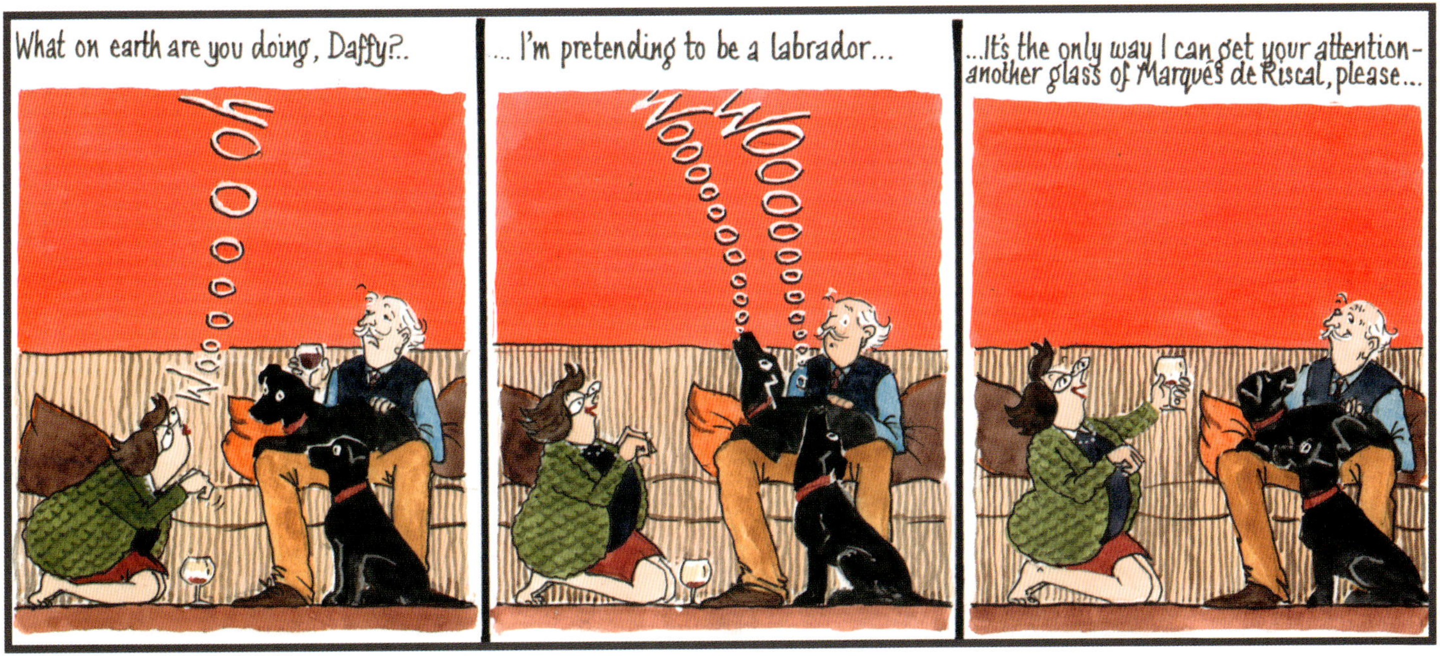
What on earth are you doing, Daffy?..
... I'm pretending to be a labrador...
...It's the only way I can get your attention-
another glass of Marqués de Riscal, please...

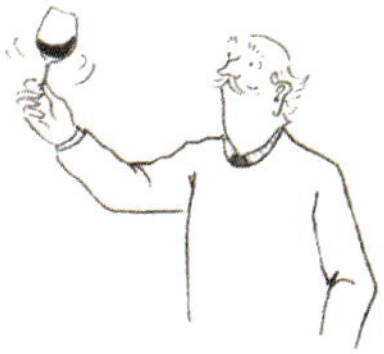

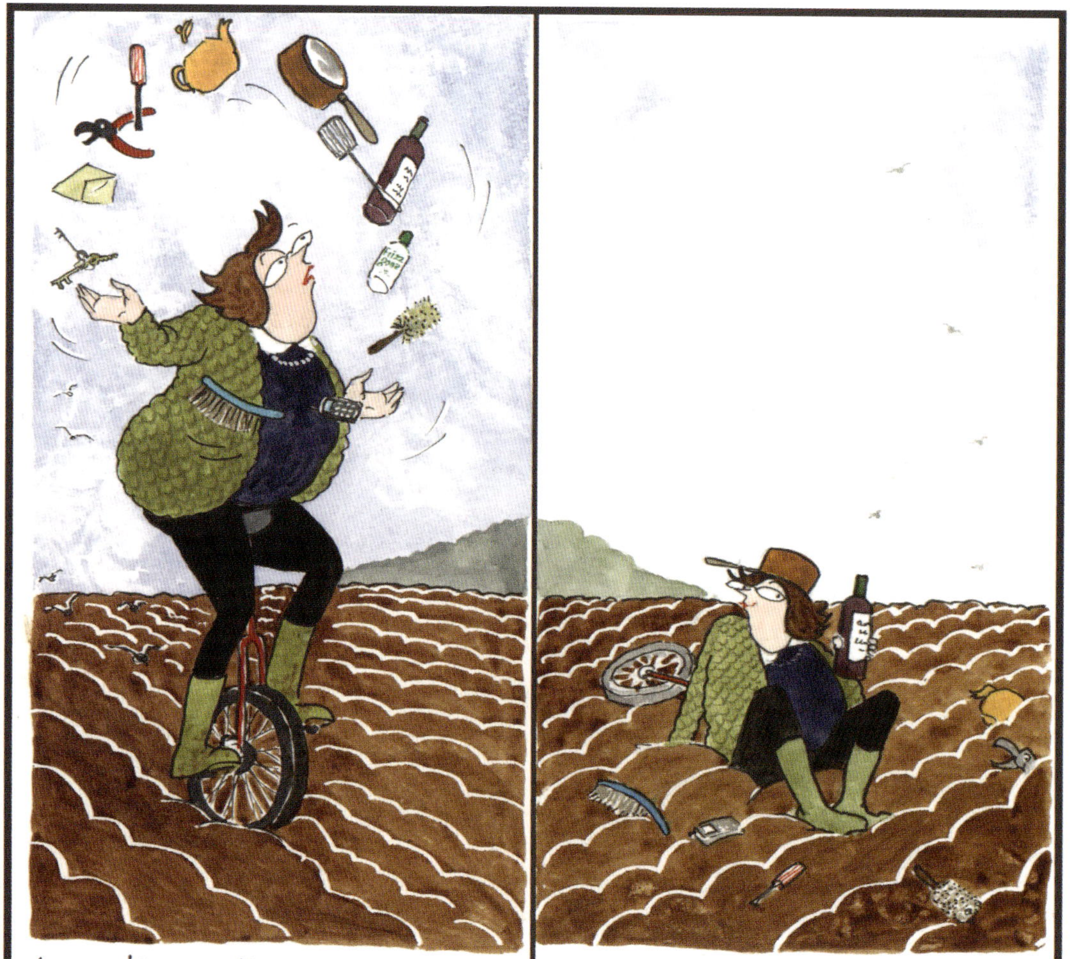

A woman's life can feel like performing a juggling act whilst riding a unicycle through a ploughed field...

Sometimes we just have to prioritise....

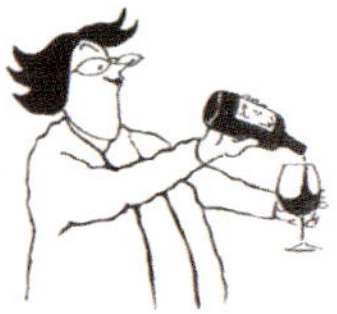

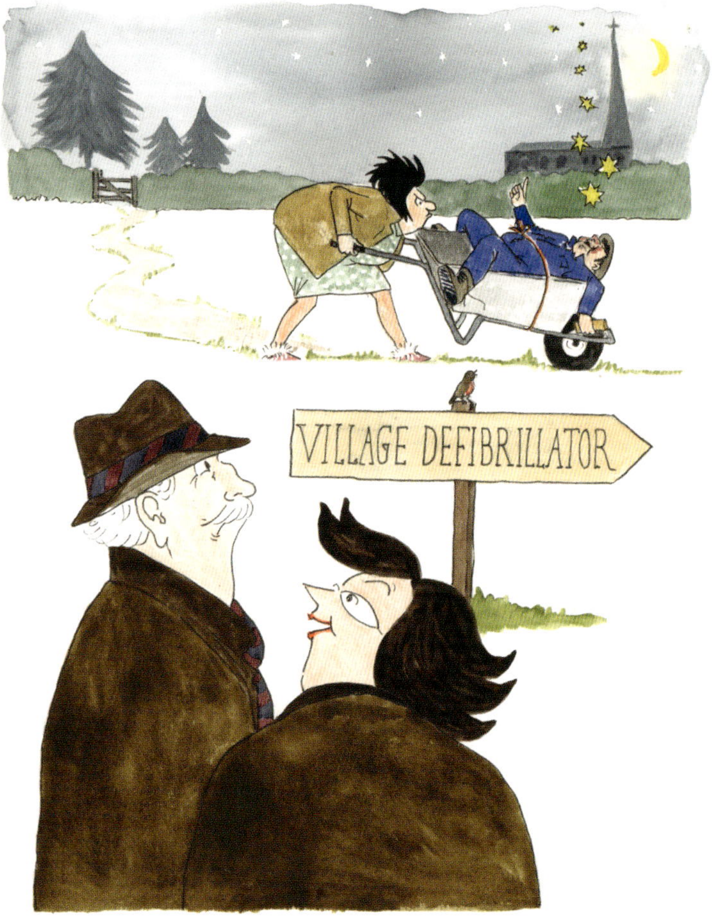
VILLAGE DEFIBRILLATOR

" Well she did warn him that if he came home drunk again she'd zap him..."

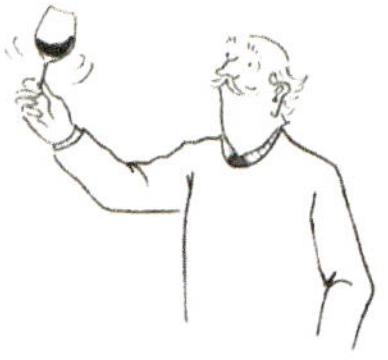

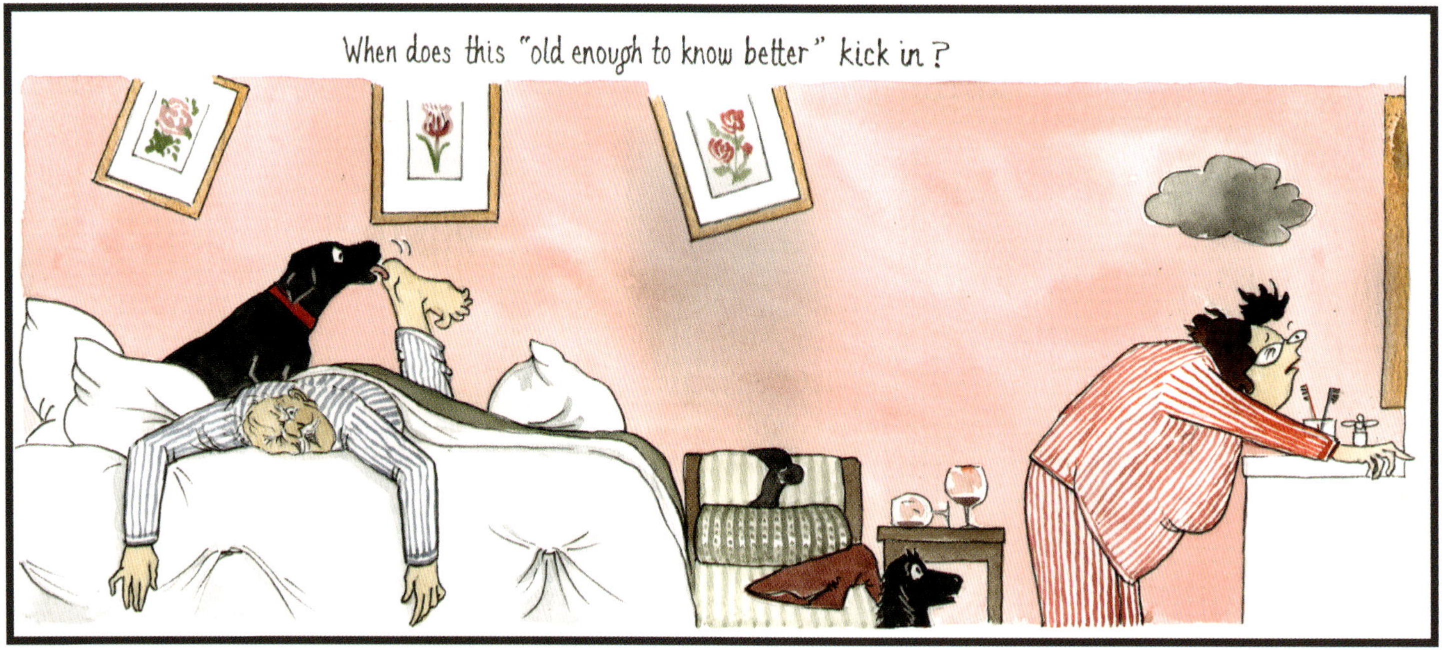

When does this "old enough to know better" kick in?

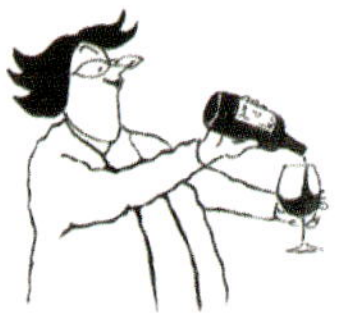

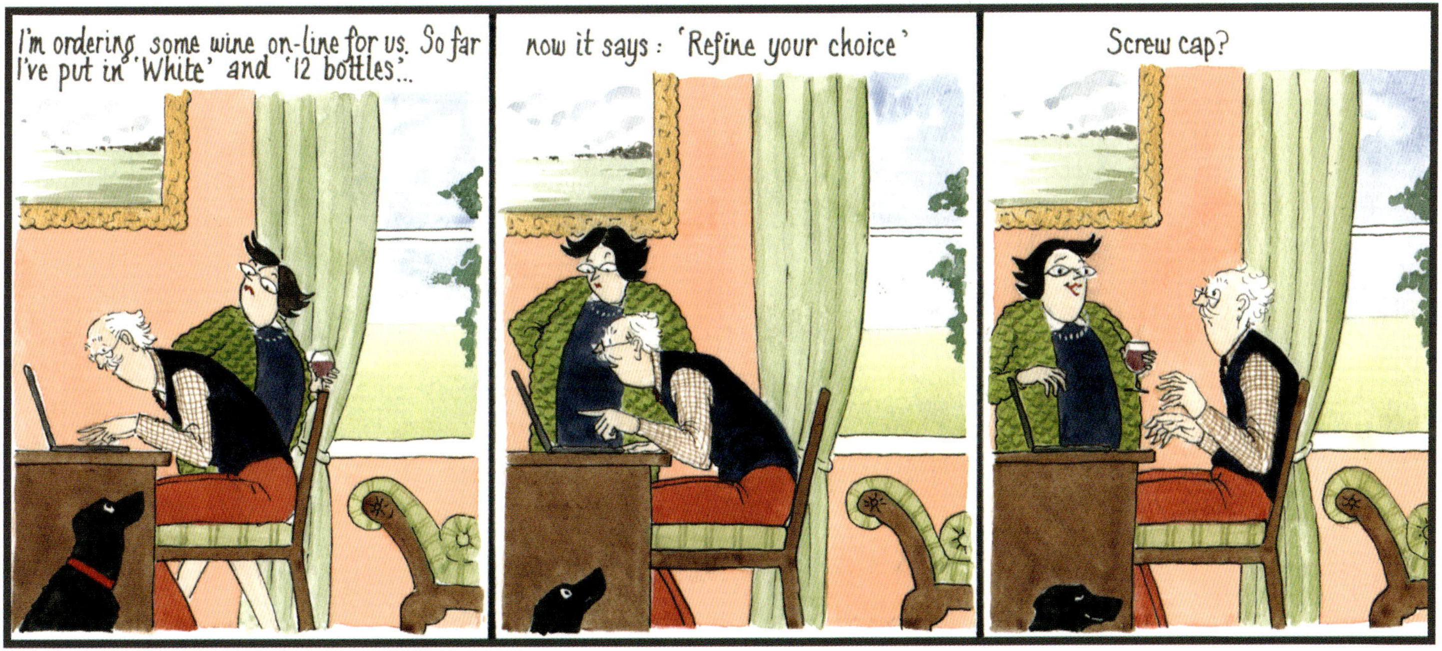
I'm ordering some wine on-line for us. So far I've put in 'White' and '12 bottles'...
now it says: 'Refine your choice'
Screw cap?

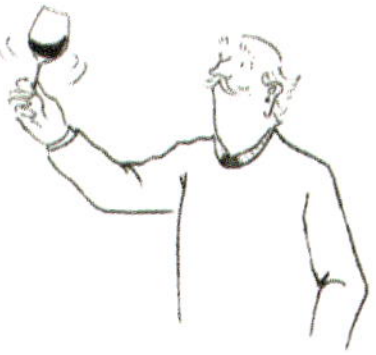

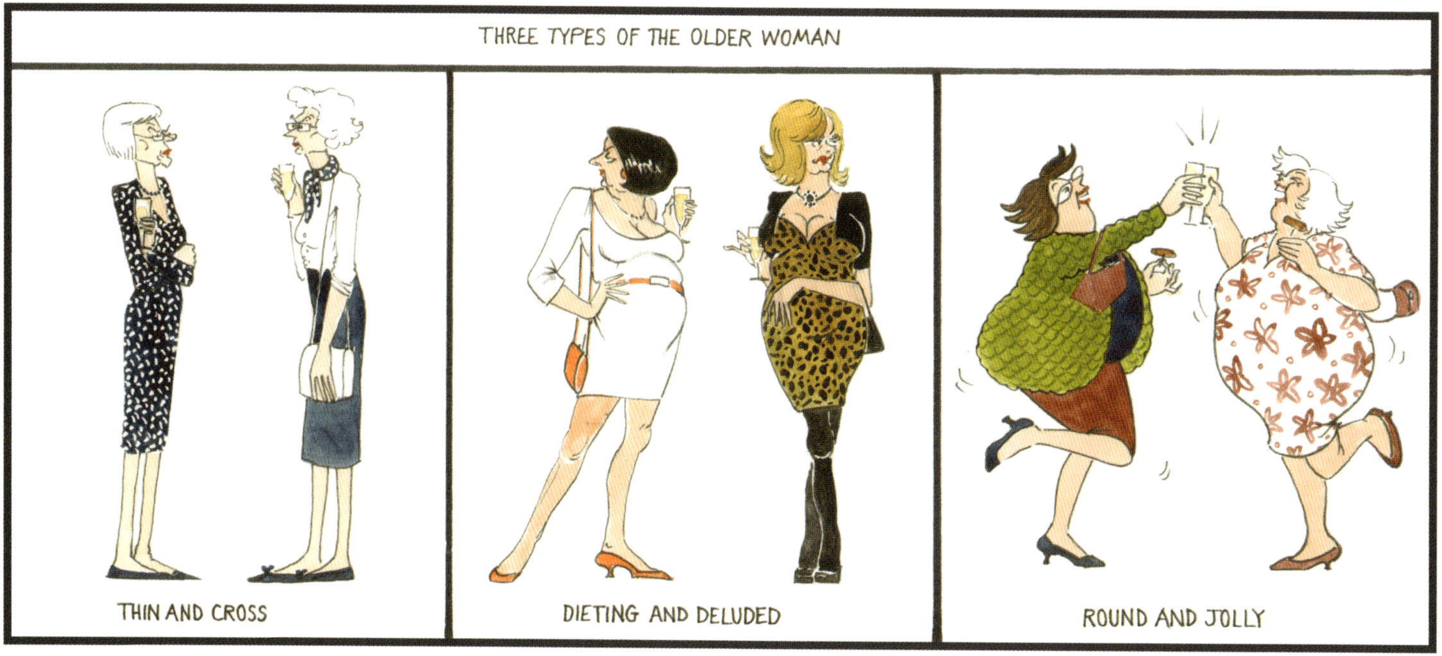
THREE TYPES OF THE OLDER WOMAN
THIN AND CROSS
DIETING AND DELUDED
ROUND AND JOLLY

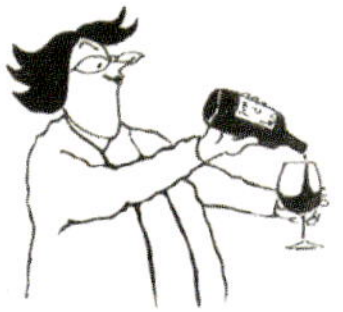

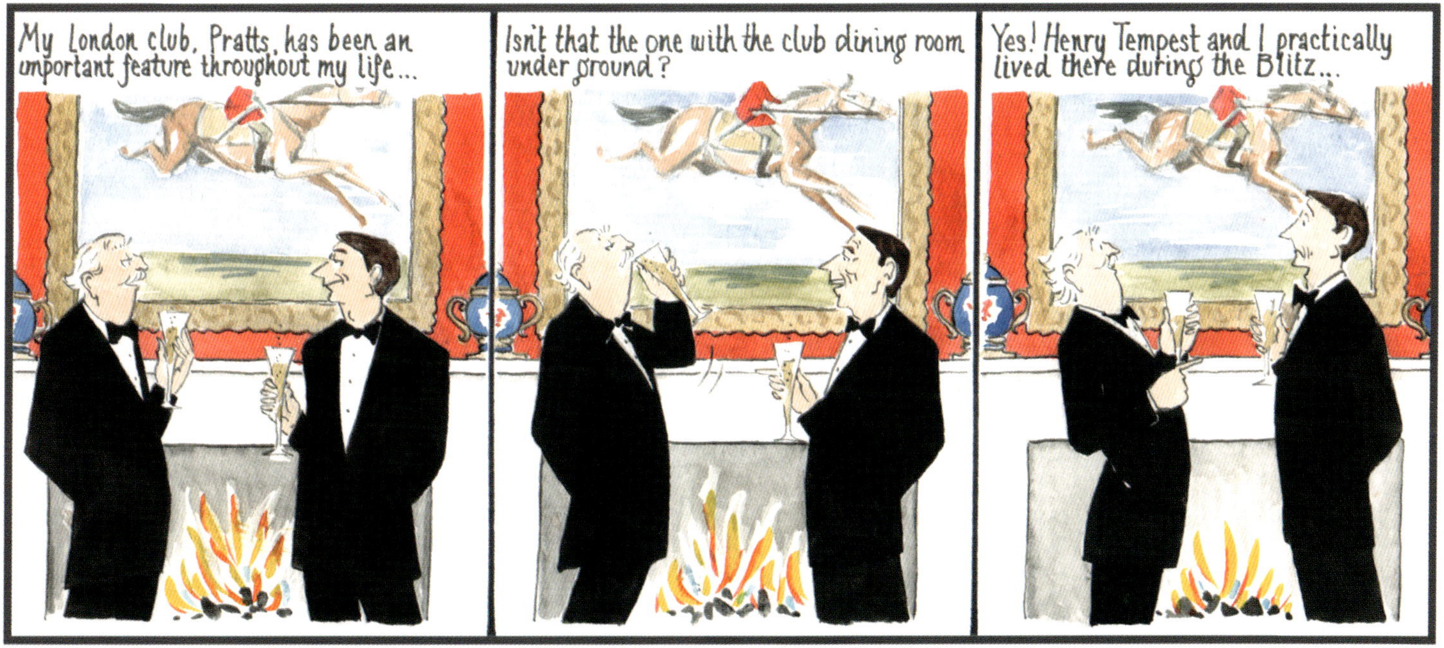
My London club, Pratts, has been an important feature throughout my life...
Isn't that the one with the club dining room under ground?
Yes! Henry Tempest and I practically lived there during the Blitz...

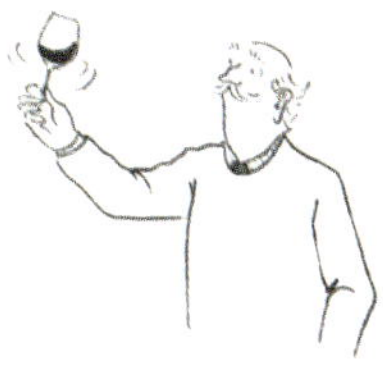

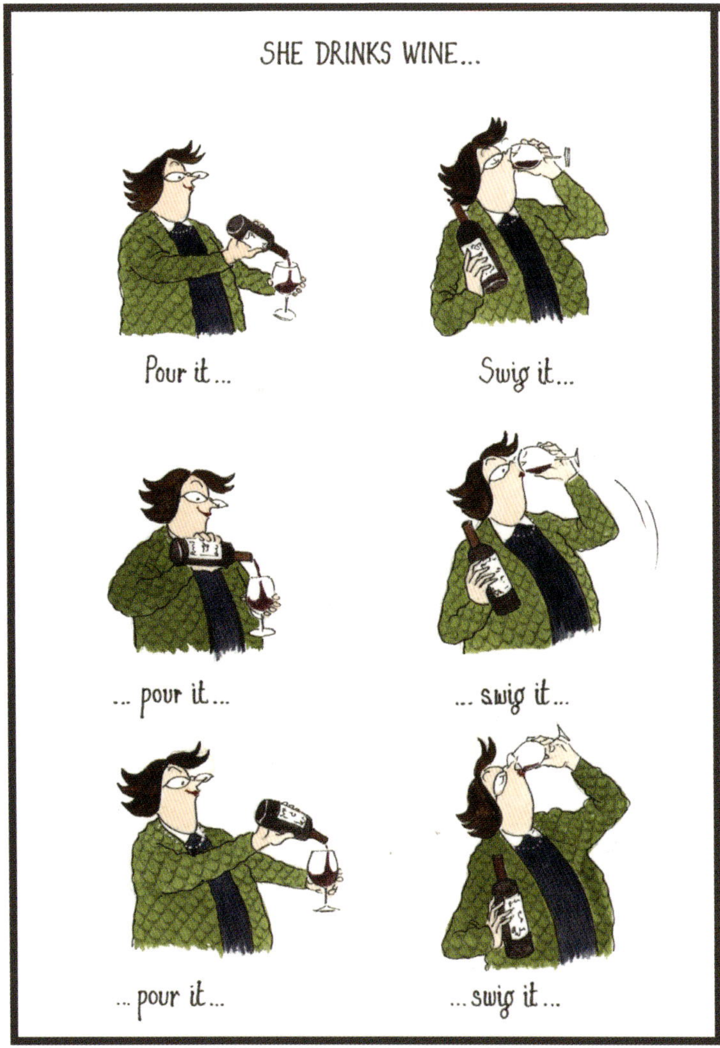
SHE DRINKS WINE...
Pour it...
Swig it...
... pour it...
... swig it...
... pour it...
... swig it...

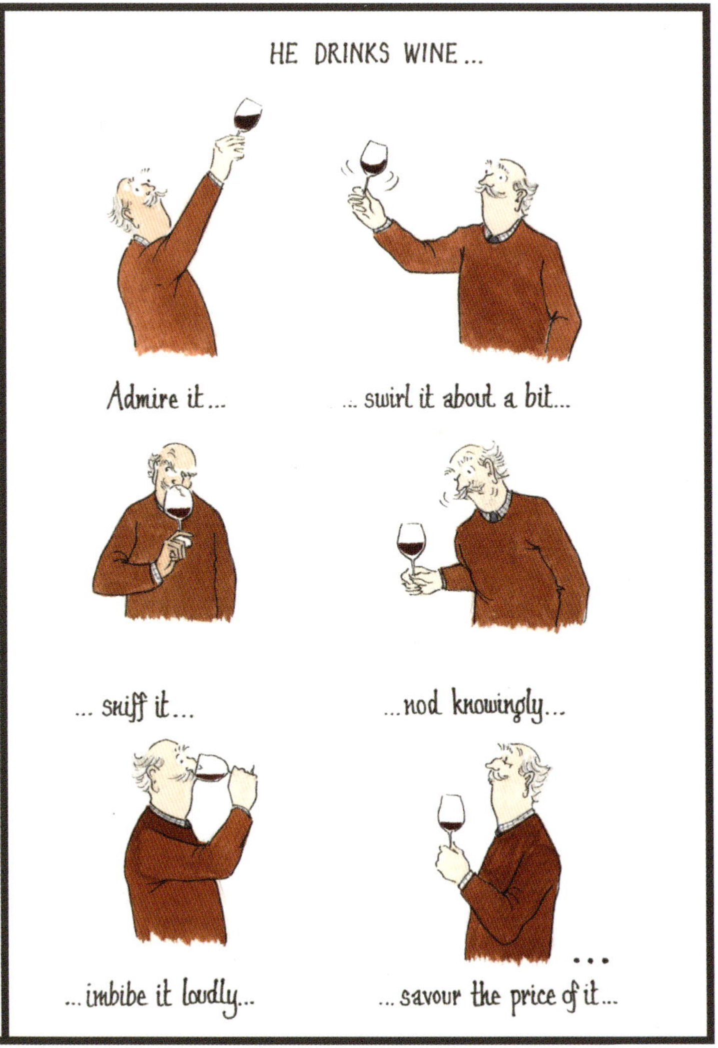
HE DRINKS WINE...
Admire it...
... swirl it about a bit...
... sniff it...
... nod knowingly...
... imbibe it loudly...
... savour the price of it...

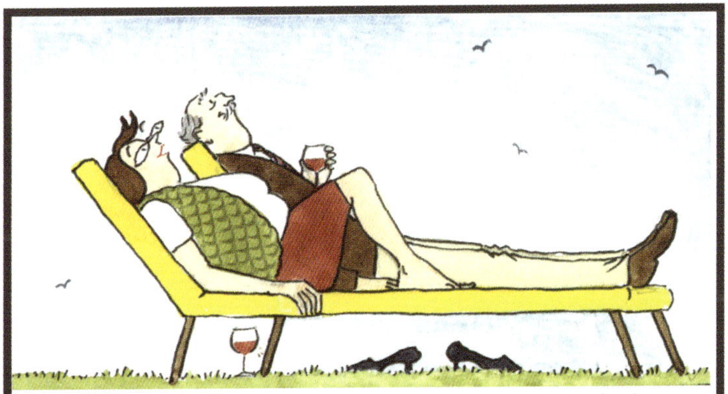

What a perfect day! The sun is out and so are the kids...

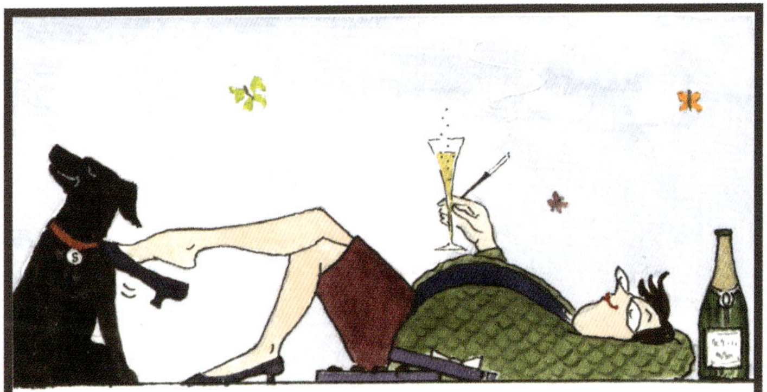

THE FEMALE CHARACTER
A talent for multitasking, even when at rest...

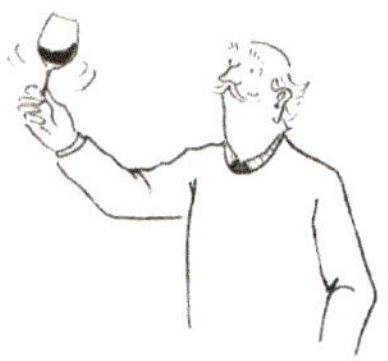

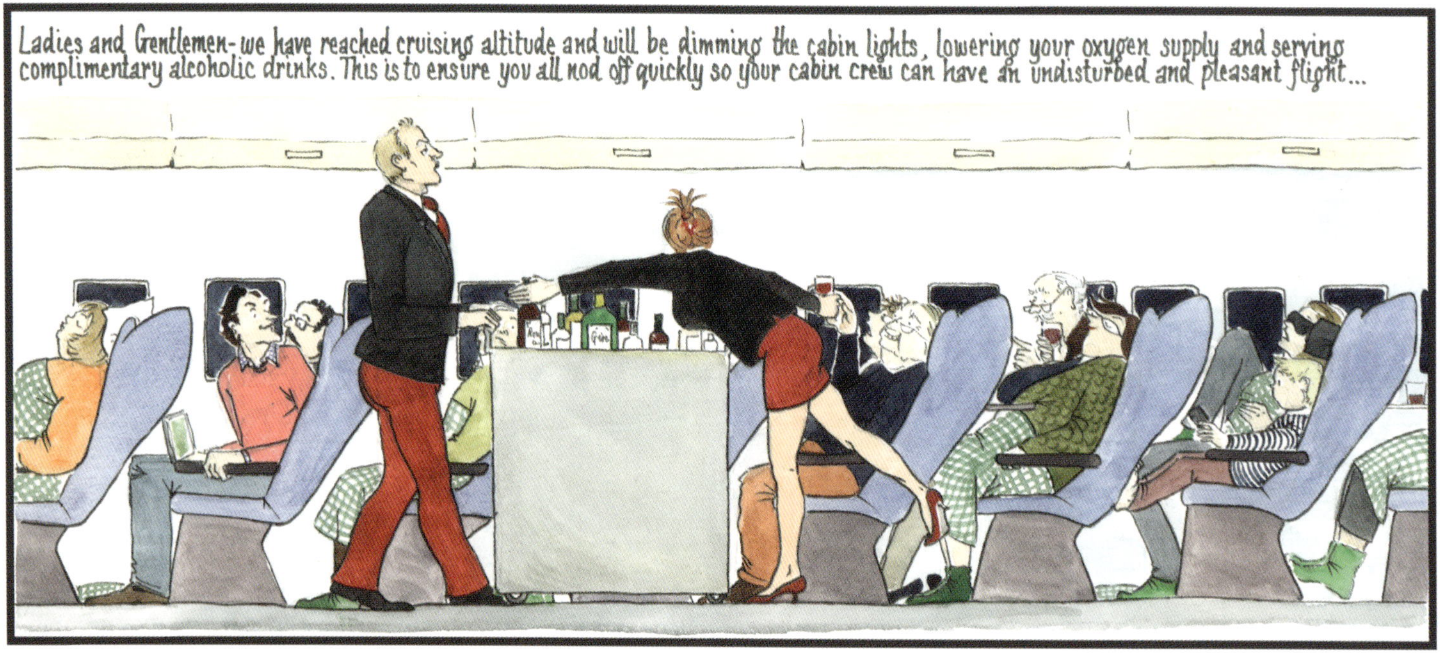
Ladies and Gentlemen- we have reached cruising altitude and will be dimming the cabin lights, lowering your oxygen supply and serving complimentary alcoholic drinks. This is to ensure you all nod off quickly so your cabin crew can have an undisturbed and pleasant flight...

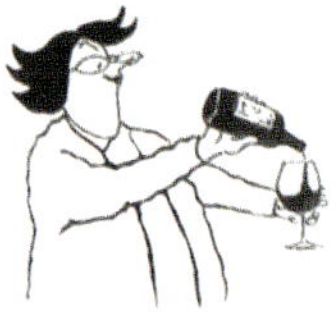

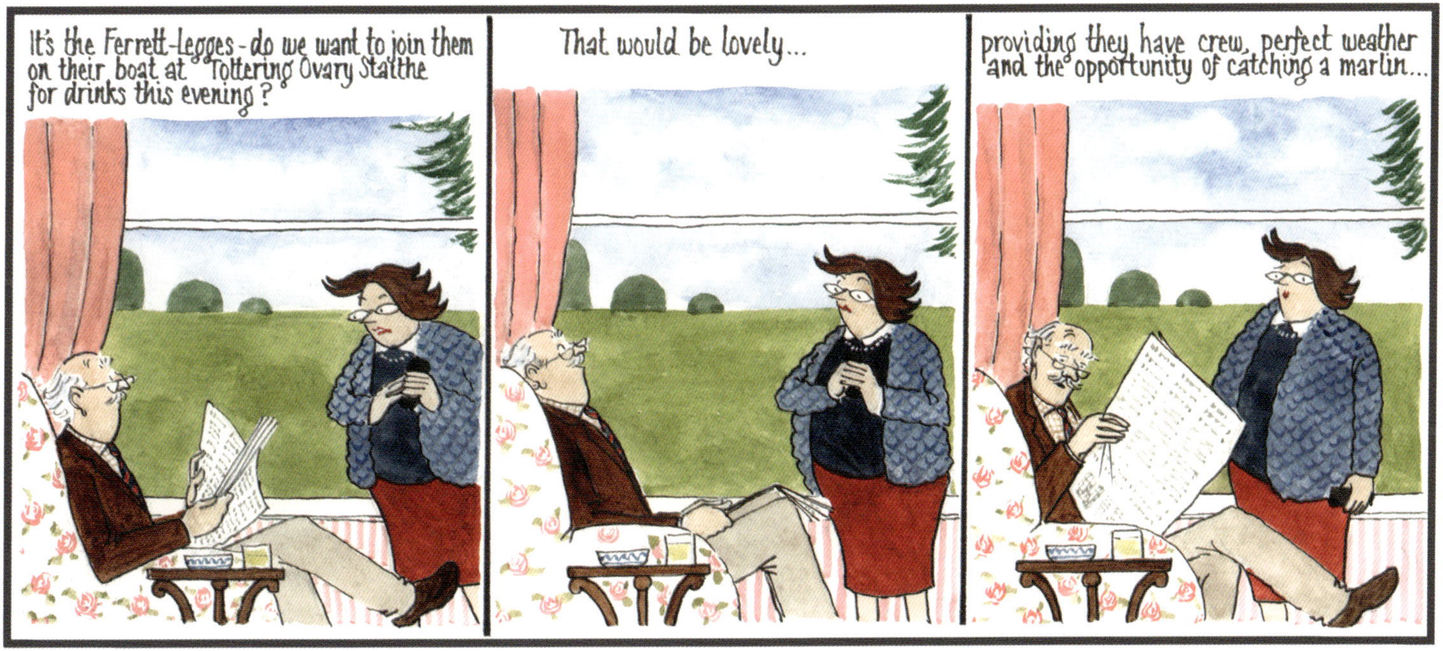
It's the Ferrett-Legges - do we want to join them on their boat at Tottering Ovary Staithe for drinks this evening?
That would be lovely...
providing they have crew, perfect weather and the opportunity of catching a marlin...

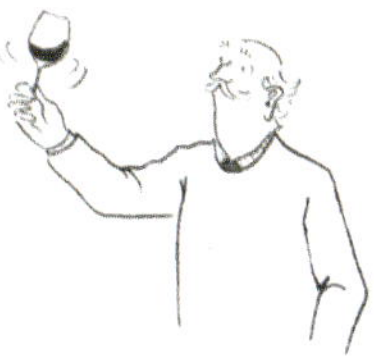

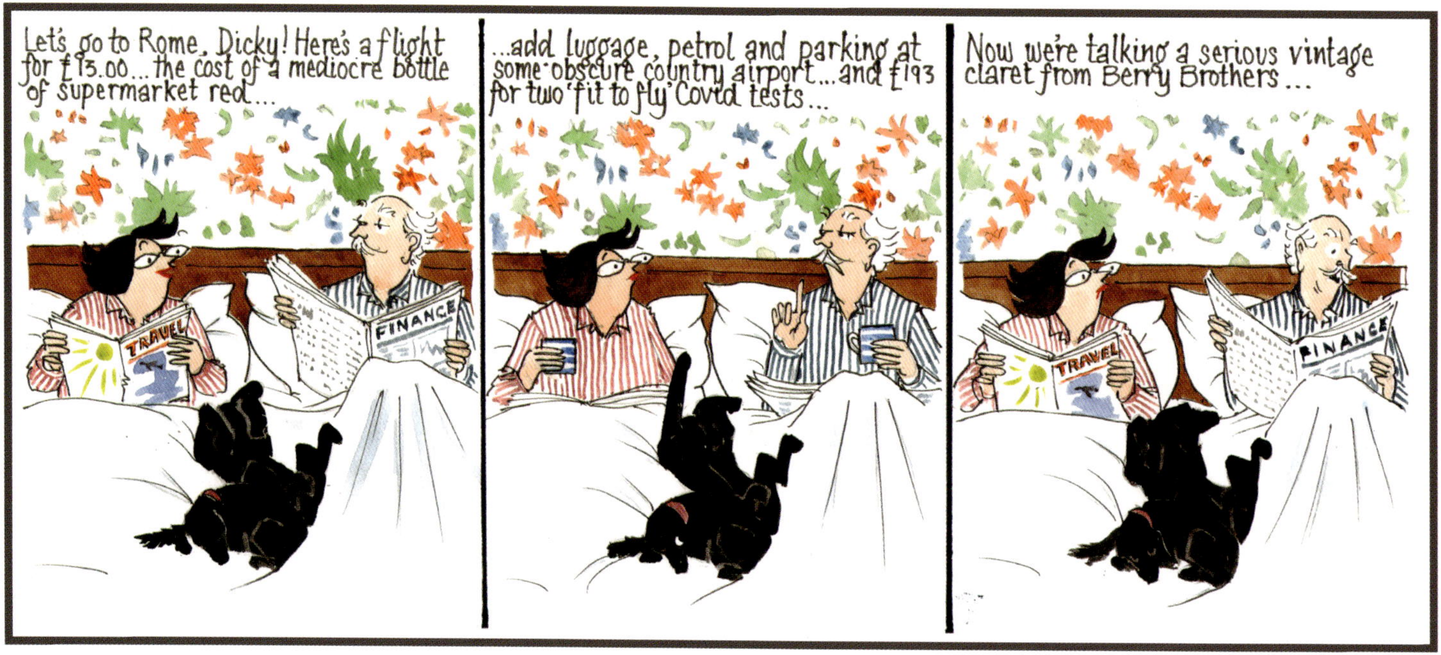
Let's go to Rome, Dicky! Here's a flight for £13.00... the cost of a mediocre bottle of supermarket red...
TRAVEL
FINANCE
...add luggage, petrol and parking at some obscure country airport... and £193 for two 'fit to fly' Covid tests...
Now we're talking a serious vintage claret from Berry Brothers...
TRAVEL
FINANCE

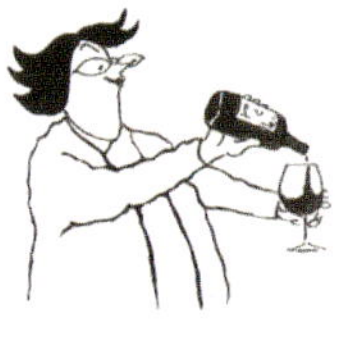

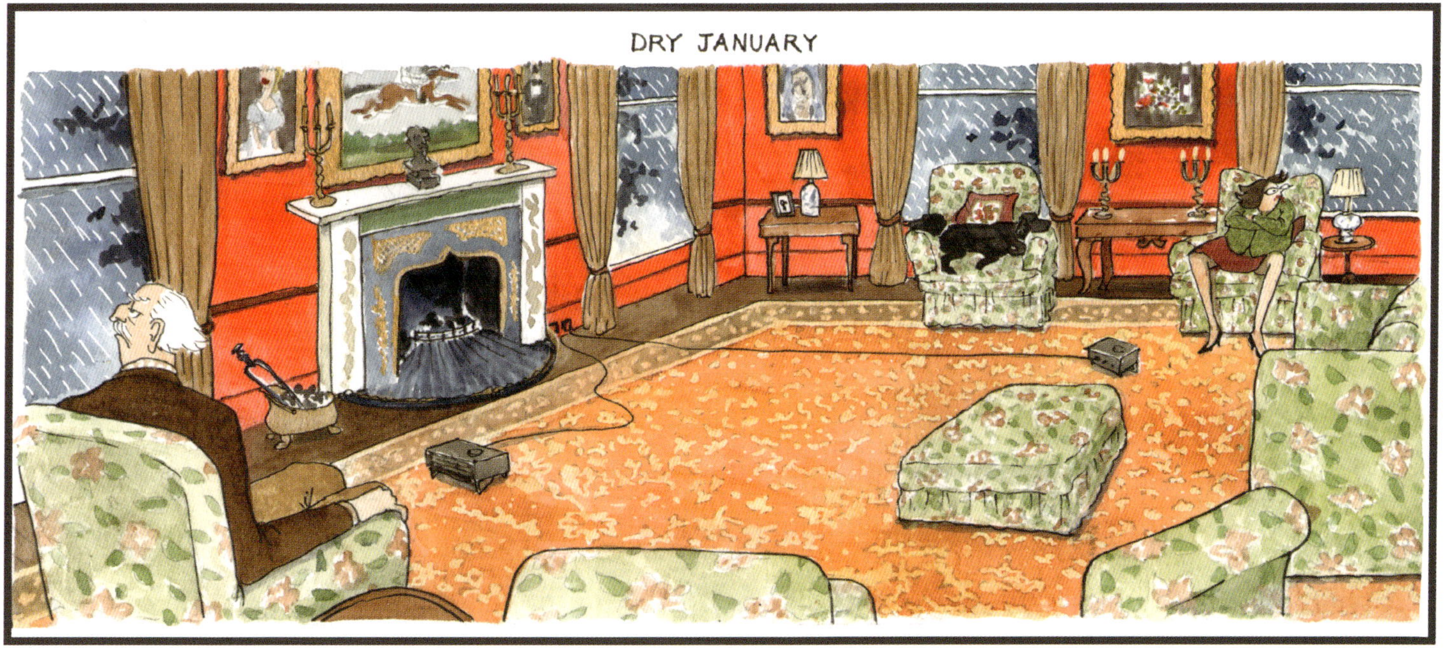

DRY JANUARY

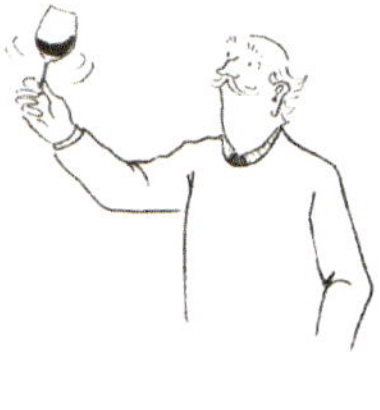

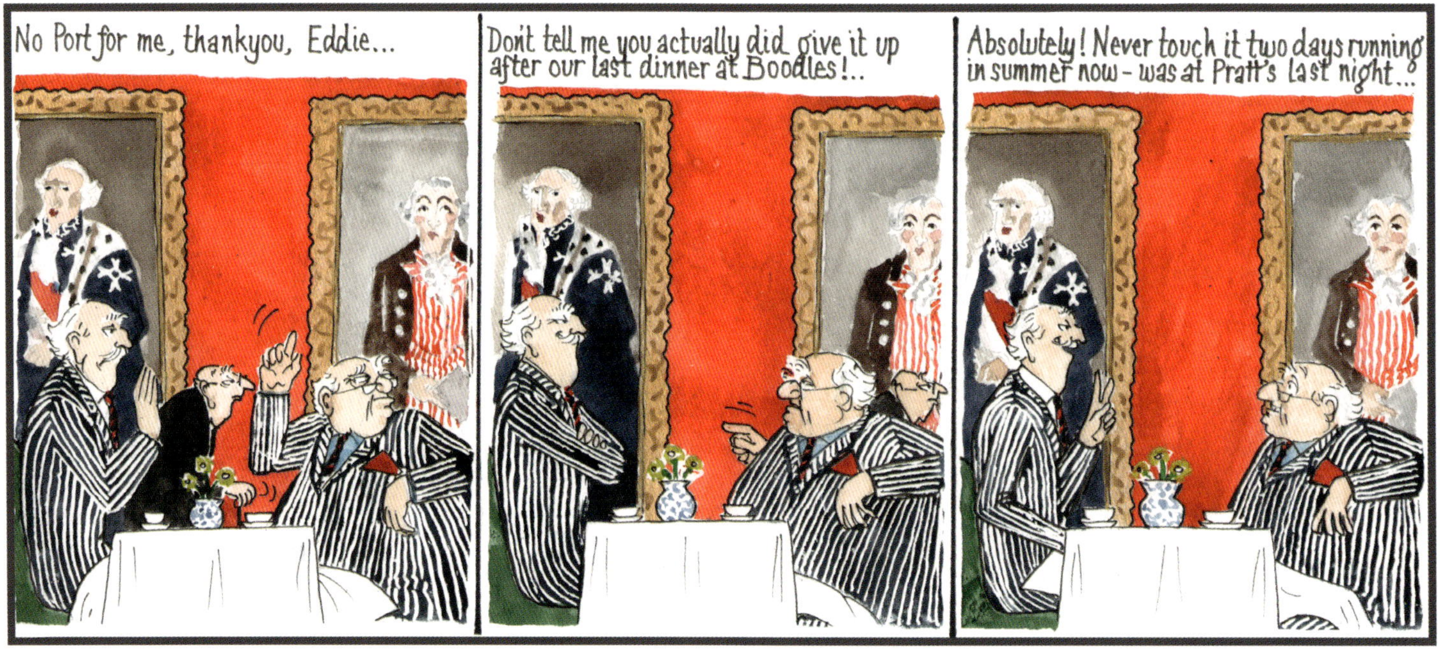
No Port for me, thankyou, Eddie...
Don't tell me you actually did give it up after our last dinner at Boodles!..
Absolutely! Never touch it two days running in summer now - was at Pratt's last night...

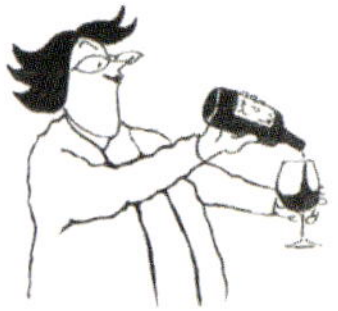

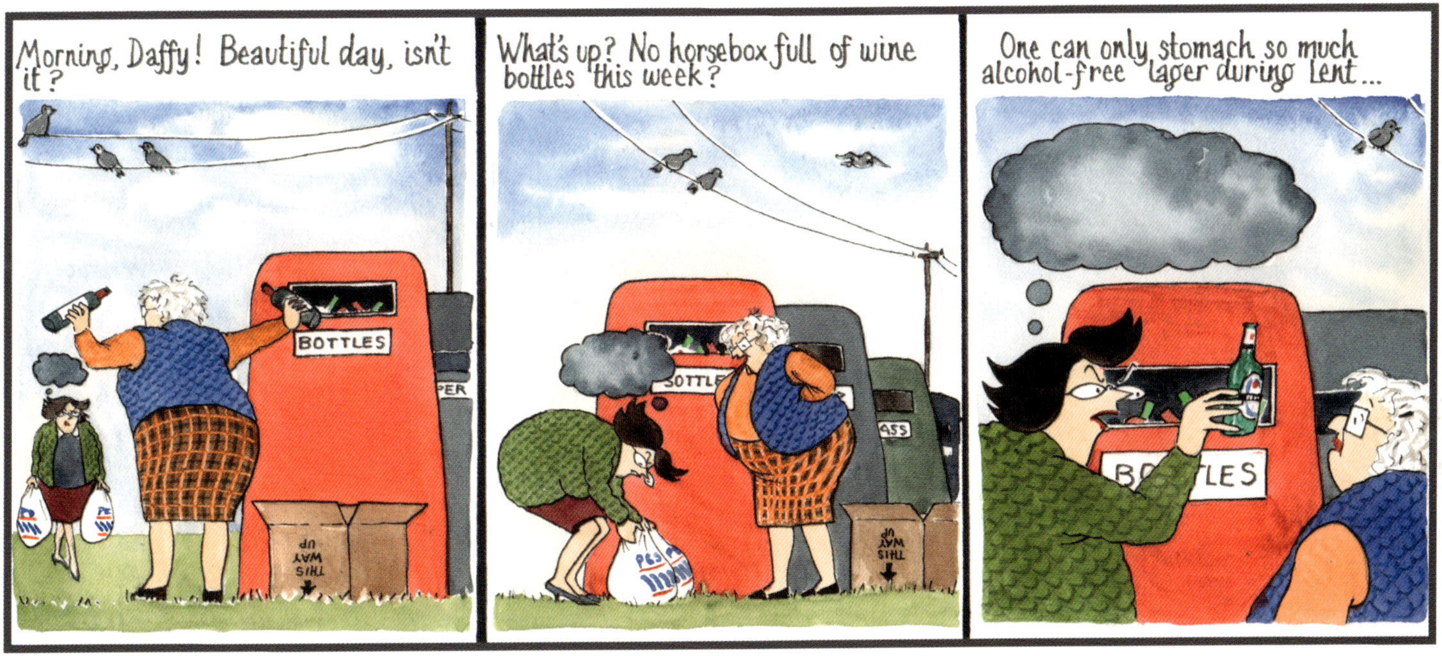
Morning, Daffy! Beautiful day, isn't it?
BOTTLES
What's up? No horsebox full of wine bottles this week?
One can only stomach so much alcohol-free lager during Lent...

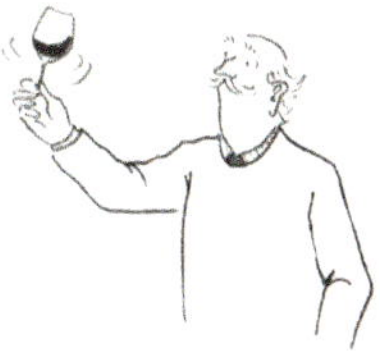

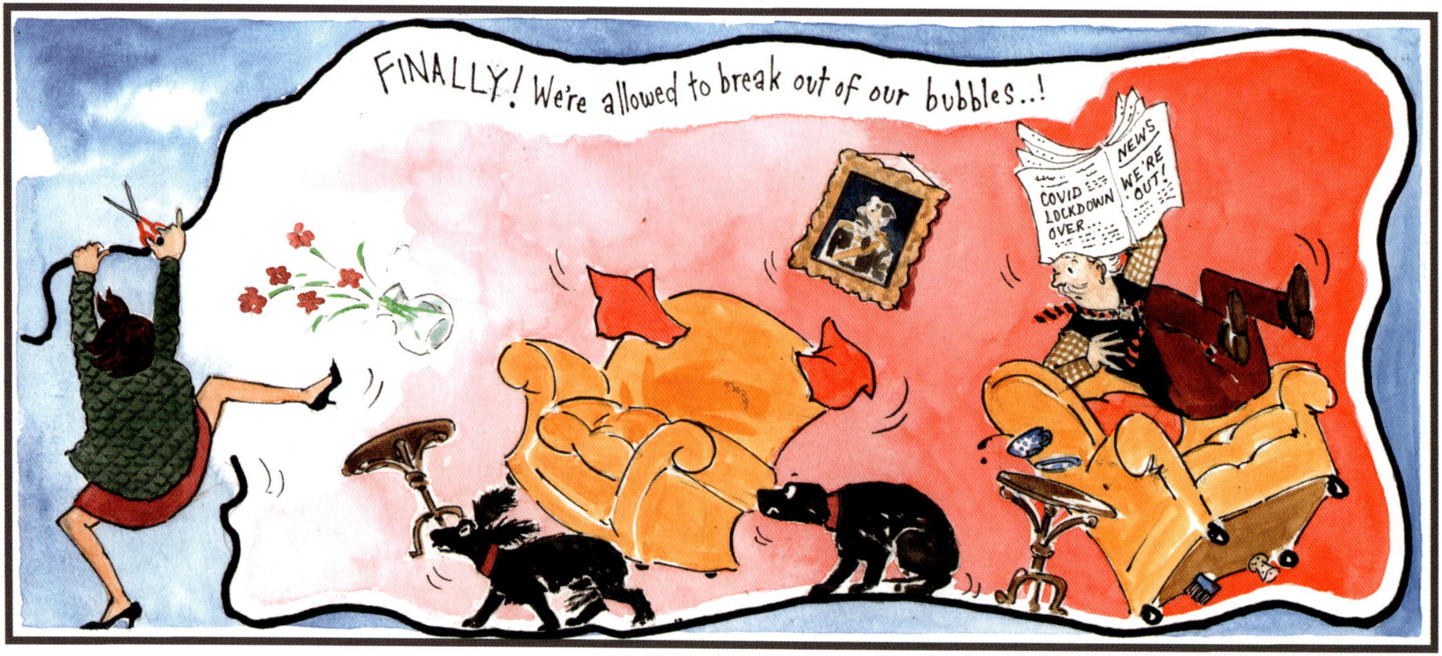
FINALLY! We're allowed to break out of our bubbles..!
NEWS
COVID LOCKDOWN OVER...
WE'RE OUT!

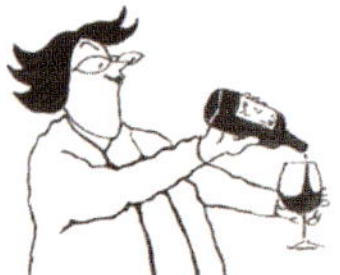

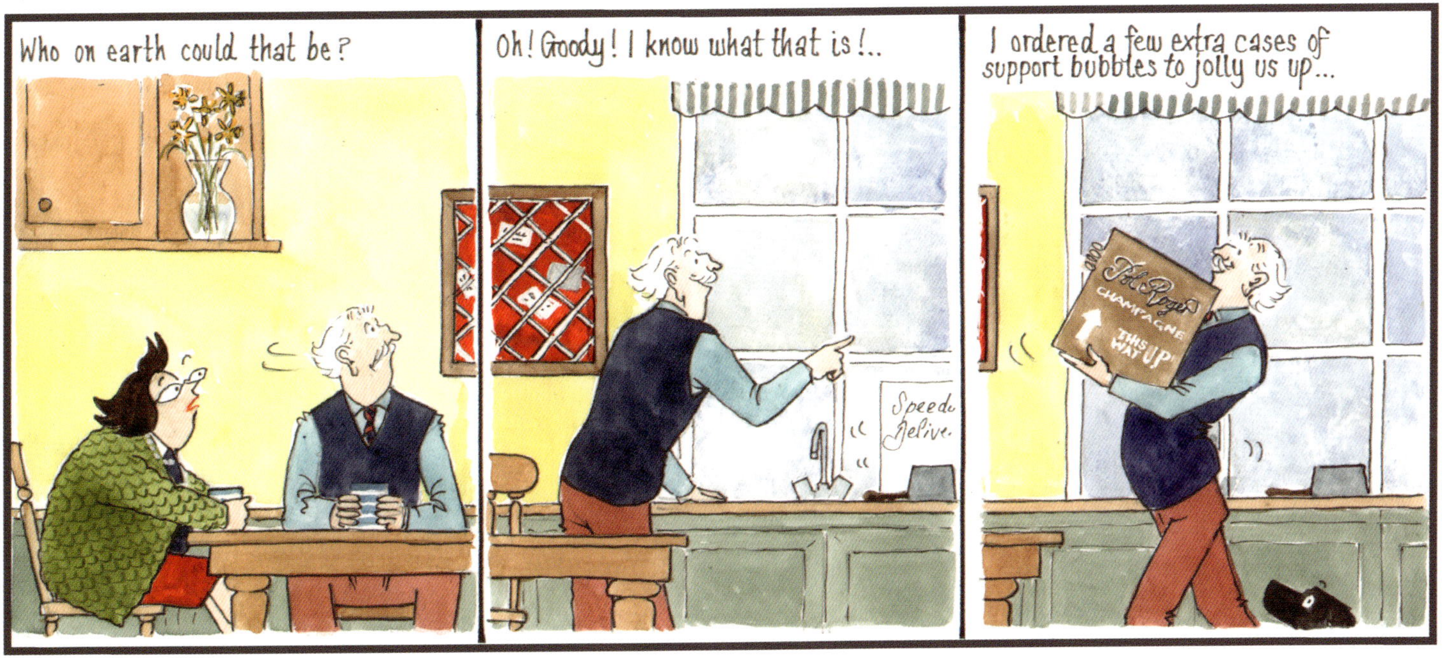
Who on earth could that be?
Oh! Goody! I know what that is!..
I ordered a few extra cases of support bubbles to jolly us up...
Pol Roger
CHAMPAGNE
THIS WAY UP!

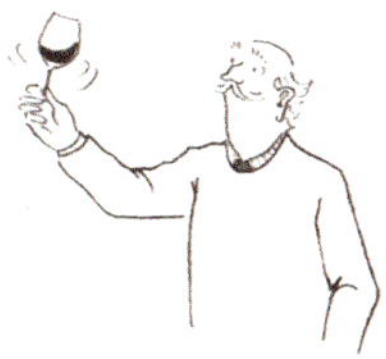

Excuse me! If we have some Moët bottles and some Veuve Clicquot - does that make them mixed glass?..

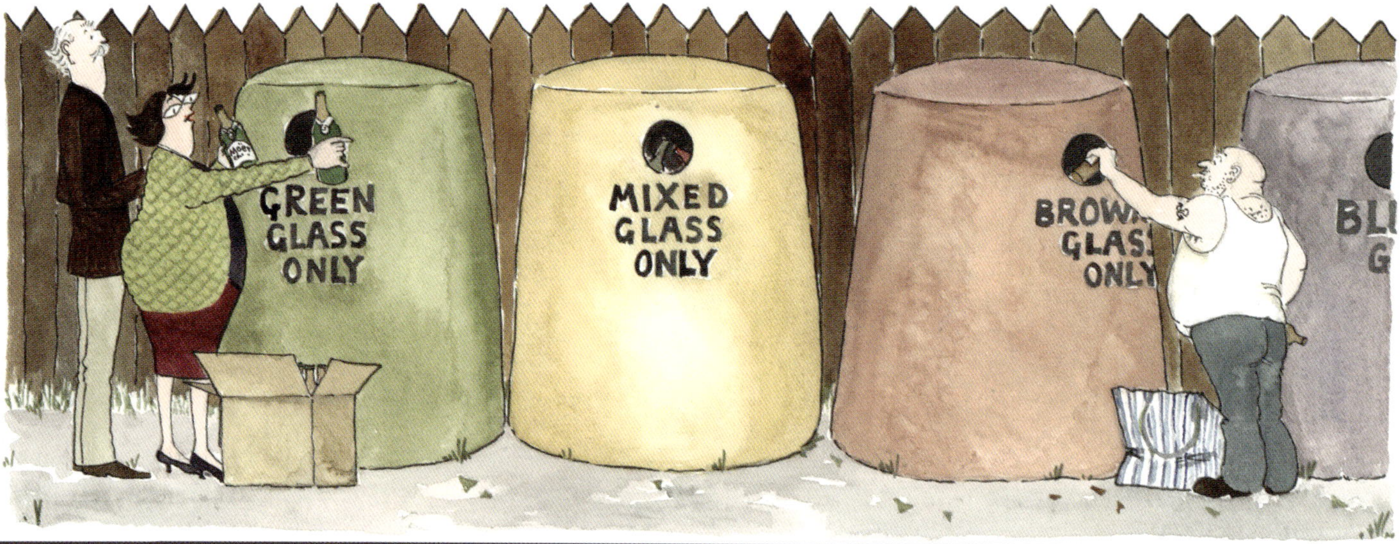
GREEN GLASS ONLY
MIXED GLASS ONLY

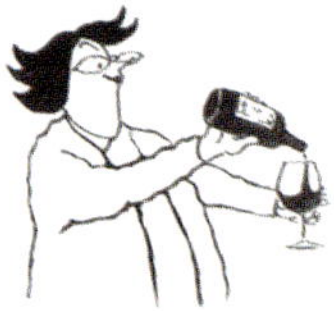

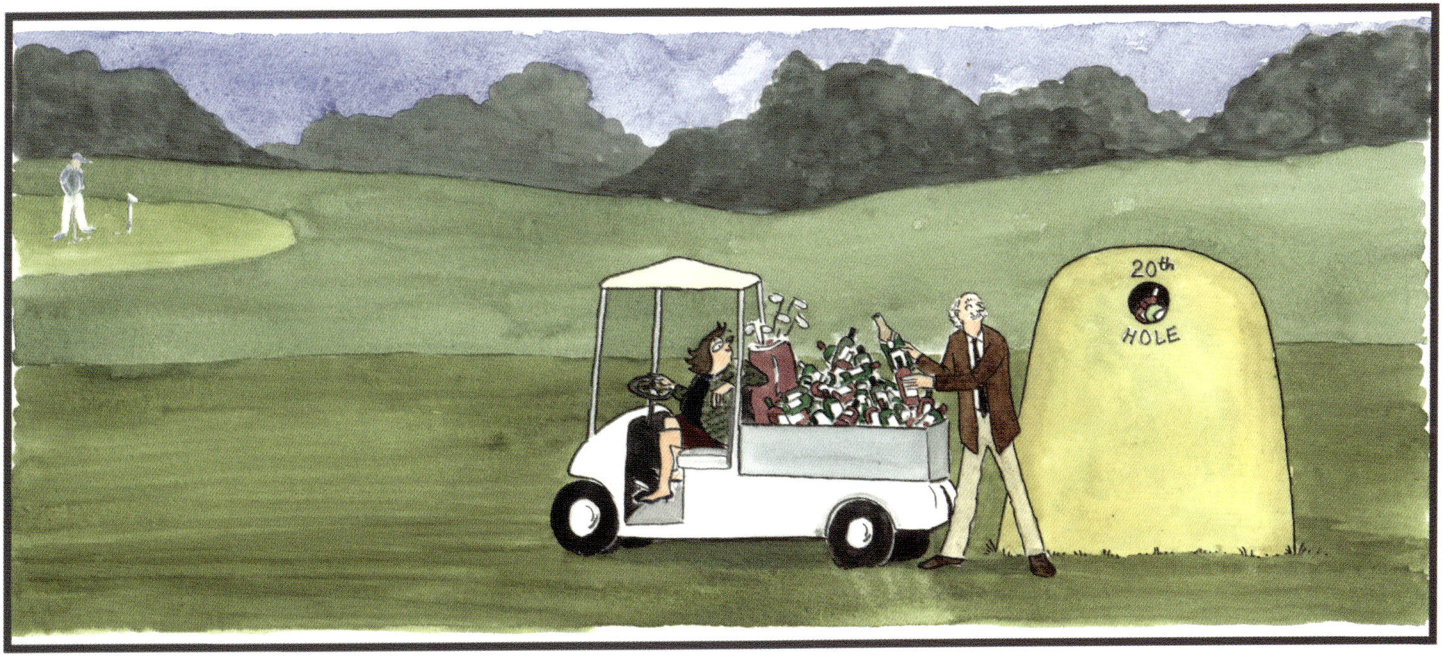
20th
HOLE

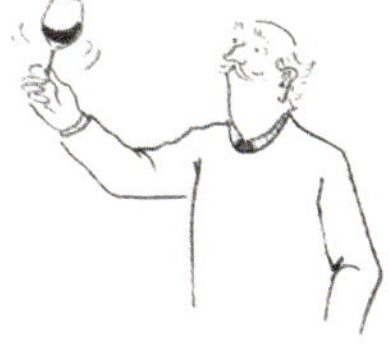

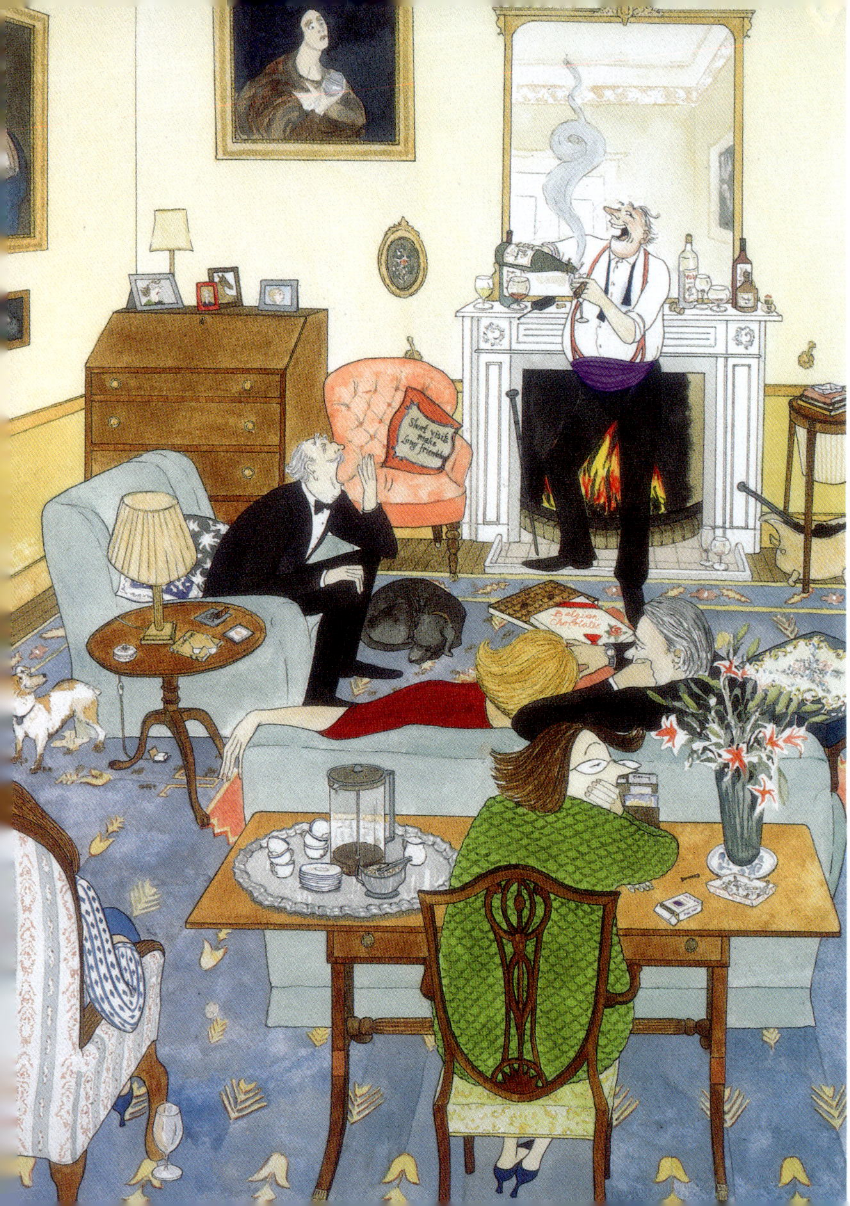
Short visits
make
long
Belgian
Chocolates

The guest from hell

DAFFY'S DAILY

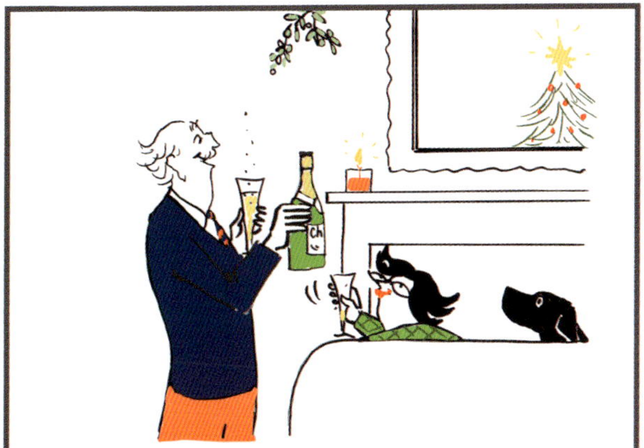

"Anyone for another glass of support bubbles?...

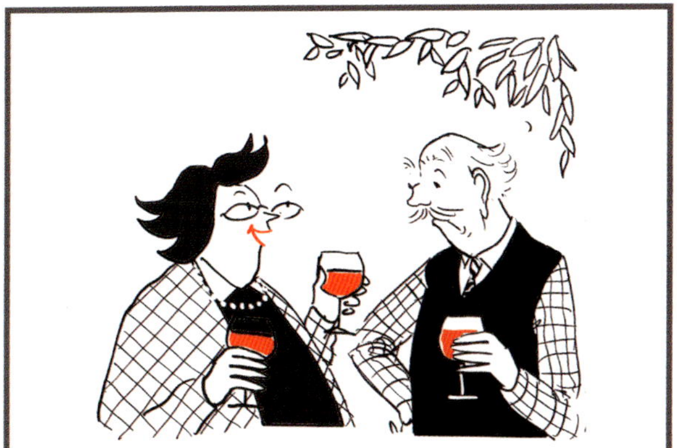

"It's just that I find having two glasses of wine
At once stops me touching my face..."

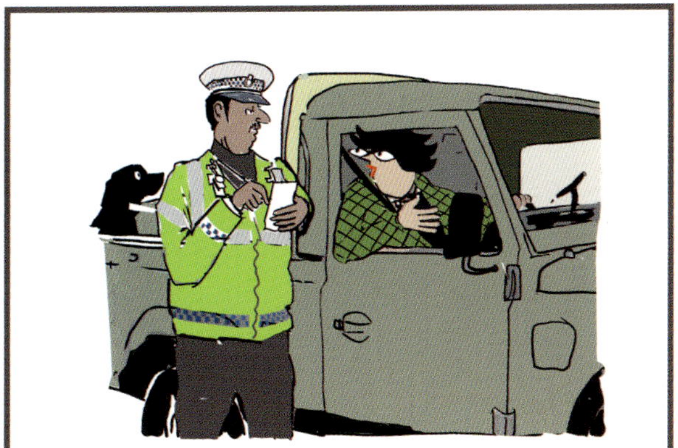

"It is alcohol you can smell, officer...it's my hand
sanitiser..."

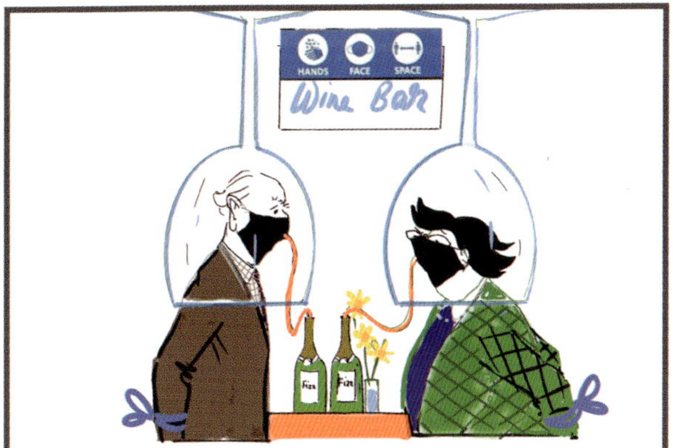
HANDS
FACE
SPACE
Wine Bar
Fizz
Fizz

"Happy anniversary, darling...This is as romantic as I'm allowed
to be..."

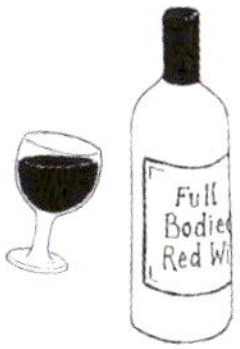

DAFFY'S DAILY

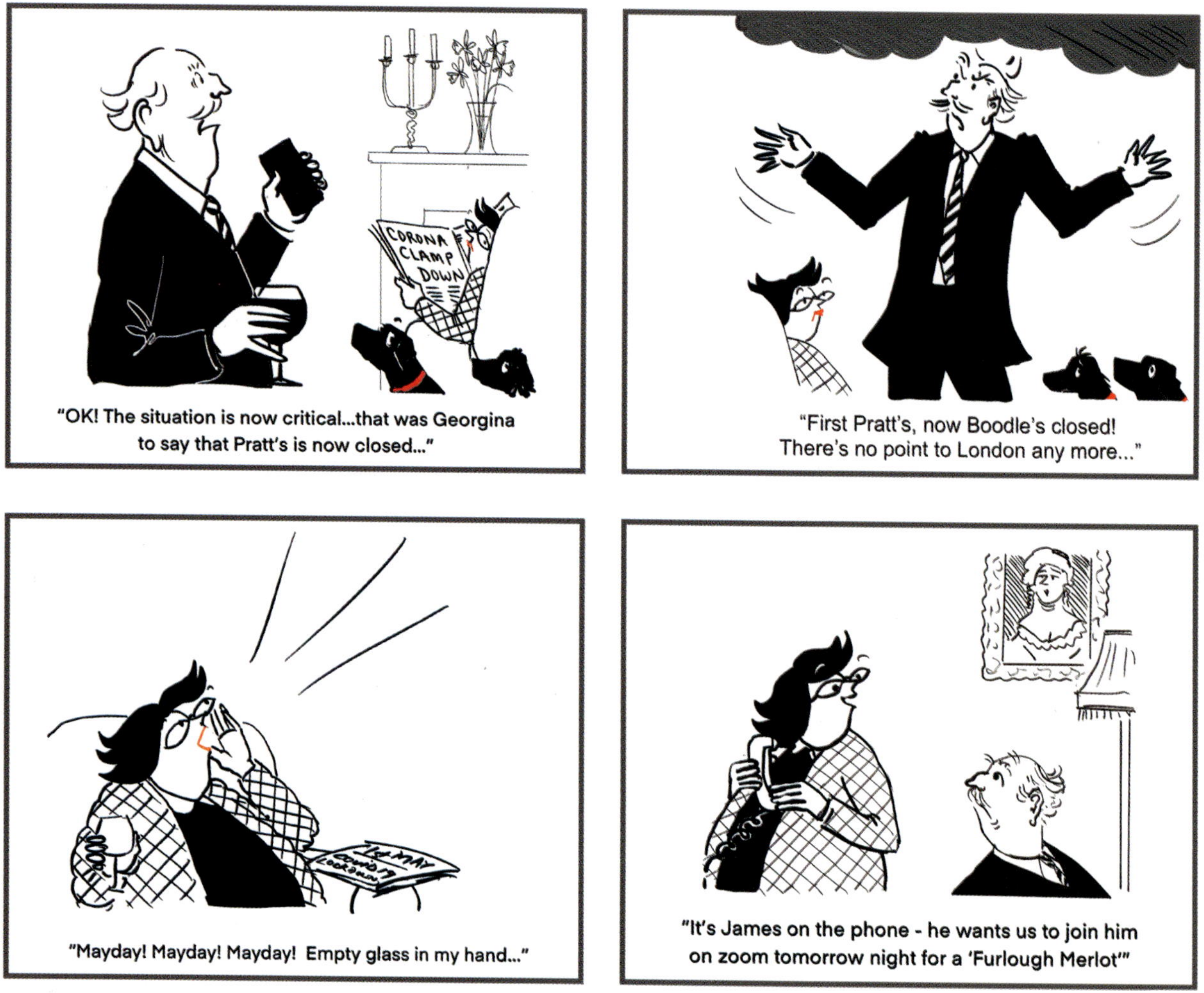
CORONA CLAMP DOWN
"OK! The situation is now critical...that was Georgina to say that Pratt's is now closed..."
"First Pratt's, now Boodle's closed! There's no point to London any more..."
"Mayday! Mayday! Mayday! Empty glass in my hand..."
"It's James on the phone - he wants us to join him on zoom tomorrow night for a 'Furlough Merlot'"

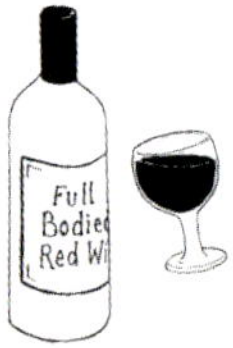

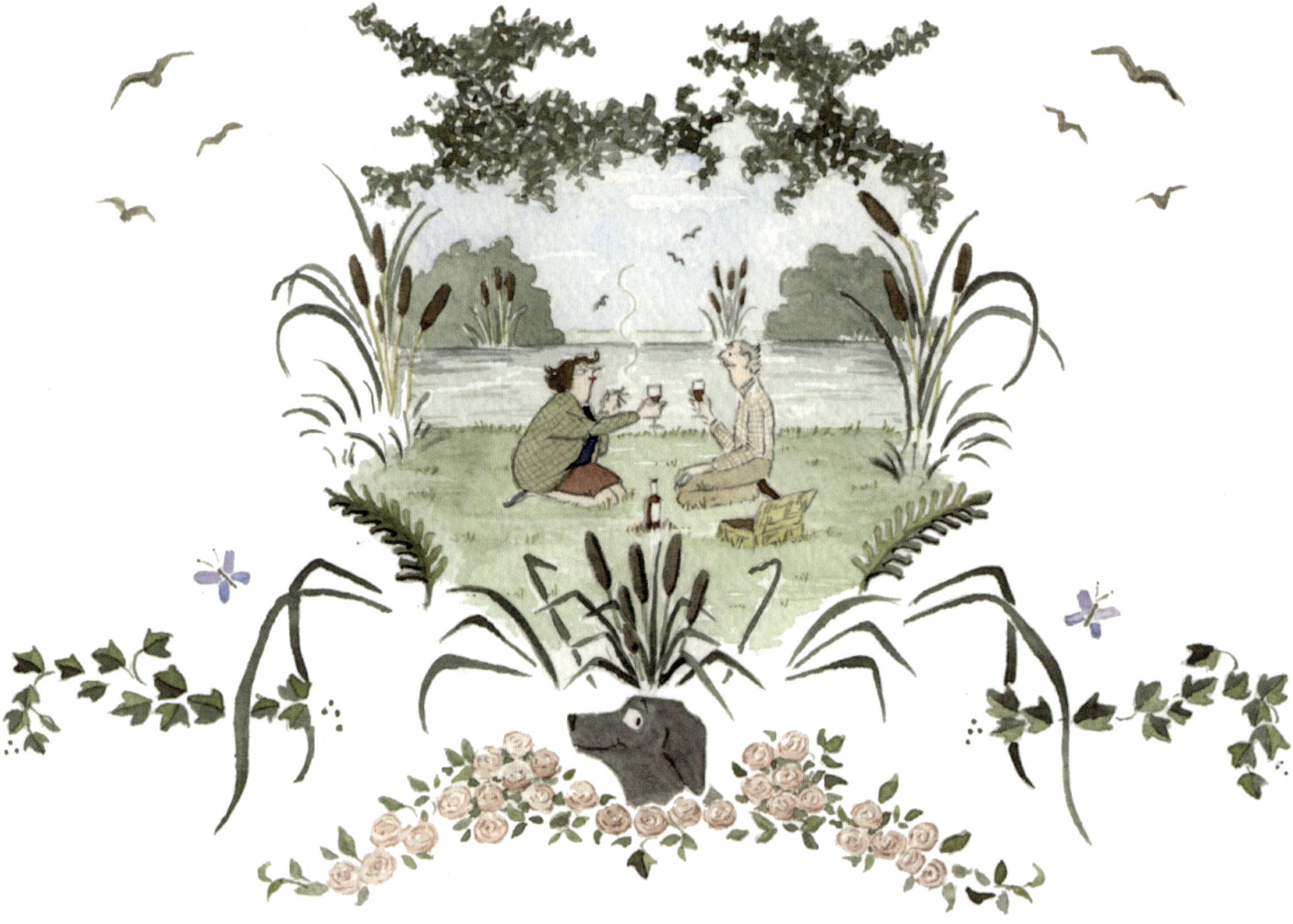